Exploring Gun Use
in America

Exploring Gun Use in America

VOLUME 3

Children and Guns

GREENWOOD PRESS
Westport, Connecticut · London

Library of Congress Cataloging-in-Publication Data

Exploring gun use in America / Creative Media Applications.
      p. cm. — (Middle school reference)
    Includes bibliographical references and index.
    Contents: v. 1. The second amendment — v. 2. The firearms industry —
  v. 3. Children and guns — v. 4. Public opinion.
    ISBN 0-313-32896-X (alk. paper: set) — ISBN 0-313-32897-8 (alk. paper: vol. 1) —
    ISBN 0-313-32898-6 (alk. paper: vol. 2) — ISBN 0-313-32899-4 (alk. paper: vol. 3) —
    ISBN 0-313-32900-1 (alk. paper: vol. 4)
        1. Gun control — United States. 2. Firearms — Law and legislation — United States.
        3. Gun control — United States — Public opinion. 4. Public opinion — United States.
    I. Creative Media Applications. II. Series.
    HV7436.E94   2004
    363.33'0973 — dc22   2003067750

British Library Cataloguing in Publication Data is available.

Copyright © 2004 by Greenwood Publishing Group, Inc.

All rights reserved. No portion of this book may be
reproduced, by any process or technique, without the
express written consent of the publisher.

Library of Congress Catalog Card Number: 2003067750
ISBN: 0-313-32896-X (set)
        0-313-32897-8 (vol. 1)
        0-313-32898-6 (vol. 2)
        0-313-32899-4 (vol. 3)
        0-313-32900-1 (vol. 4)

First published in 2004

Greenwood Press, 88 Post Road West, Westport, CT 06881
An imprint of Greenwood Publishing Group, Inc.
www.greenwood.com

Printed in the United States of America

The paper used in this book complies with the
Permanent Paper Standard issued by the National
Information Standards Organization (Z39.48–1984).

10 9 8 7 6 5 4 3 2 1

A Creative Media Applications, Inc. Production
WRITER: Mathew Kachur
DESIGN AND PRODUCTION: Alan Barnett, Inc.
EDITOR: Matt Levine
COPYEDITOR: Laurie Lieb
PROOFREADER: Betty Pessagno
INDEXER: Nara Wood
ASSOCIATED PRESS PHOTO RESEARCHER: Yvette Reyes
CONSULTANT: Eugene Volokh, Professor of Law, UCLA School of Law

PHOTO CREDITS:
AP/Wide World Photographs *pages:* vii, viii, 1, 2, 5, 6, 9, 11, 12, 15, 17, 18, 21, 23, 25, 26, 29, 30, 33, 34, 37, 39, 41, 45, 47, 48, 51,
    54, 57, 58, 61, 63, 64, 67, 69, 71, 73, 74, 77, 78, 81, 83, 84, 87, 89, 93, 95, 96, 99, 100, 103, 105, 106, 111, 112, 117, 119, 120
© Philip James Corwin/CORBIS *page:* 42
© Charles Gupton/CORBIS *page:* 90
© HAYDEN ROGER CELESTIN/EPA/Landov *page:* 109
© Jay Dickman/CORBIS *page:* 115

Table of Contents

INTRODUCTION

Children can legally use guns for hunting and for self-defense. Although people under the age of eighteen generally are not allowed to own handguns, this restriction does not seem to prevent many teenagers from having easy access to small firearms, as well as long guns such as rifles and shotguns. In a recent survey, about a third of American teens believed that if they really wanted to get a gun, they could easily acquire one. This statistic is not surprising, given that there are between 60 and 250 million guns in America and that some sort of firearm is

When properly coached, children can learn to employ and respect the safety precautions that are necessary when guns are in use. This father teaches his daughter to shoot skeet (clay targets) at a range in Shreveport, Louisiana, in a controlled and monitored setting.

Police investigate a crime scene in Kentucky on September 17, 2003, where two female teenagers, possible victims of a murder-suicide, were found slain in a car. Gun control advocates believe that stricter controls on the sales of guns to minors are only one component of a comprehensive plan needed to protect young people from the danger of firearms.

thought to be present in about 40 percent of American households.

In the year 2000, more than 28,000 Americans died as a result of gunshot wounds—about 60 percent suicides and 40 percent homicides. Of these deaths, approximately 3,000, or slightly more than 10 percent of the total, took the lives of children and adolescents aged nineteen and under. Every day in the United States, about eight children and adolescents die violent deaths from either homicide or suicide, mostly committed with some form of firearm. In addition, the Centers for Disease Control (CDC) estimates that about 18,000 people aged nineteen or younger were injured by firearms in 2000. These simple statistics call attention to the role that firearms play in the lives of many American children, but precisely what the numbers mean and what can be done to reduce them are greatly disputed.

For supporters of gun control, the high crime rate and the number of young people killed and wounded with firearms are a public health crisis. They believe that the government needs to intervene to either require safety mechanisms on firearms or restrict gun ownership. For opponents of these measures, the positive benefits of guns far outweigh the disadvantages. While the gun-related death or injury of any young person is a tragedy, gun advocacy groups feel that 3,000 deaths (more than half suicides) do not constitute an emergency that requires limitations on gun ownership. They believe that the proposed limitations on gun ownership will do little to prevent these homicides and suicides, but will seriously interfere with self-defense.

The dispute over kids with guns took on added meaning in the 1980s and 1990s. From about 1983 to 1995, the United States probably experienced a greater level of lethal youth violence—especially murder—than at any time in its history. This violence killed young victims, shattered urban communities, and ruined the lives of many people across the nation. Just as the crime rate began decreasing in the late 1990s, a wave of horrifying school shootings in suburban and rural areas shocked the nation, bringing the debate over the role of guns and children in American society to national attention.

Many people agree that the safe storage of firearms is critically important. Adults must take the responsibility to make sure that guns are not left unlocked and loaded where children can get them. Only slightly more controversial is the idea of changing the design of guns to prevent firearms injuries among teenagers and younger children. Modified product designs, such as children's car seats and childproof caps on medicine bottles, now protect children from car accidents and poisoning. Similarly, safety features for firearms, such as loaded chamber indicators and magazine disconnect devices, could reduce unintentional firearm injuries. New technologies, such as "smart guns," could prevent unauthorized users of any age from firing firearms and might reduce access to firearms by adolescents.

The protection of children is not only an obligation of adults, but also an extremely powerful political appeal, especially because it allows adults to put their beliefs on the side of childlike innocence and goodness. As the firearms-related homicide rate rose (especially among teenagers and young adults) and the number of school shootings multiplied, many critics attacked American movies, television, music, and video games for glamorizing violence. Caught between freedom of speech and censorship, Americans struggled to find a workable solution for the popularity of guns and violence in entertainment aimed at children.

The entertainment industry, like the gun industry, remains controversial in the United States; for some, it is the explanation for the high rate of violence in America, while for others, it is the scapegoat for far more complex problems. Nonetheless, young people, whether as operators of guns, victims of guns, or consumers of violent entertainment, have become a major element in all debates over the role of guns in America.

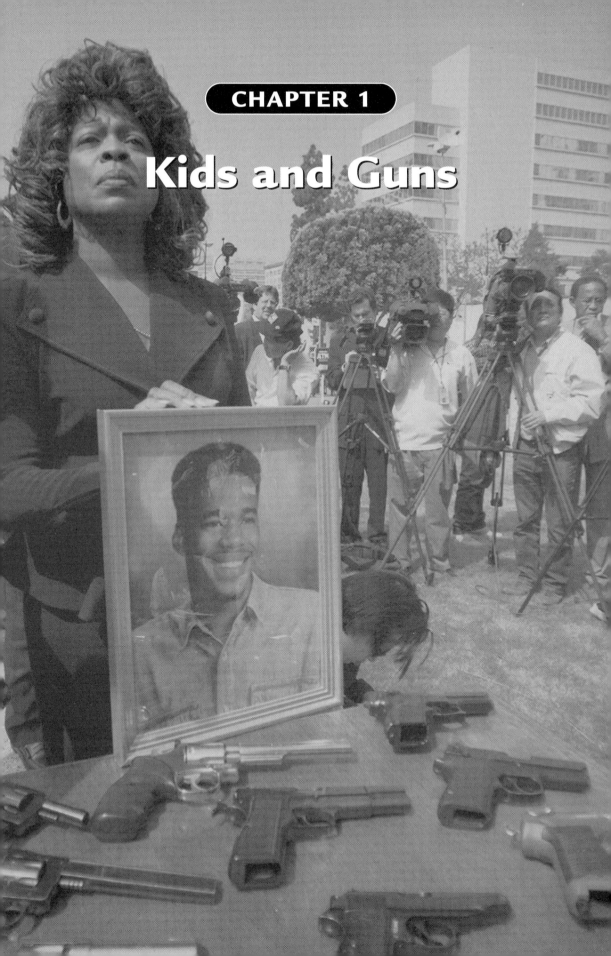

CHAPTER 1

Kids and Guns

According to American law, parents do not have absolute control over their children, even when the children are under a certain age. In the United States, children are usually assumed to possess the basic rights stated in the Constitution. The Bill of Rights (the first ten amendments to the Constitution) and the equal protection clause of the Fourteenth Amendment (which in most cases applies the Bill of Rights to state laws) apply to minors.

Nonetheless, children receive special protections in the name of maintaining their safety. American law assumes that all small children are irresponsible, at least by adult standards, and even teenagers are often considered unable to legally make contracts, regardless of the opinions of their parents or the local community. Federal, state, and local governments have all passed legislation restricting the sale of alcoholic beverages and cigarettes to minors and regulating their sexual life. Even a parent's religious beliefs must give way if they endanger the welfare of a child. Laws dictate how long children must attend school; other laws restrict where children can work and for how

Civil rights leader Reverend Al Sharpton leads a demonstration outside the courthouse in Oakland County, Michigan. Sharpton was protesting the conviction of a thirteen-year-old boy who had committed murder with a firearm when he was eleven years old. Although a minor, Nathaniel Abraham was tried as an adult, focusing attention on the difficult nature of legislating what it means legally to be a "child."

long. If they commit crimes, they are subject to different standards and judicial punishments than adults.

One problem with protecting the interests of children is that there is no strict definition of the word *child*. Does the term *children* include adolescents, and if so, to what age? This question pertains to both making laws and enforcing them. For example, in October 1997, an eleven-year-old boy borrowed a rifle and shot and killed a stranger near a convenience store in Pontiac, Michigan. In 2000, the boy officially became one of the youngest murderers in American history, charged with homicide under a 1997 Michigan law that allows children of any age to be prosecuted as adults for serious crimes. However, a six-year-old who shot a classmate in Mount Morris, Michigan, was not tried under the same law. The prosecutor said, "If you're under a certain age, you can't form the mental intentions to appreciate the consequences of your actions sufficiently enough to be criminally responsible. There's not much I can do to him [the six-year-old], other than make sure he's safe and in an environment where he's not inclined to do such hazardous behavior."

Arguments about children and guns often use different age brackets, depending on what point they want to prove; some supporters of fewer restrictions on gun ownership even deny that teenagers are children. Obviously, the capabilities of a five-year-old, a twelve-year-old, and a seventeen-year-old vary a great deal. Different degrees of responsibility depend upon different stages of development, but there is no agreement at all as to when a child is old enough to responsibly handle a gun. It is the job of adults, both in their role as parents and as citizens working through legislators, to make these decisions.

The Law Restricts Children and Guns

Legislatures often make laws protecting young people, regardless of their individual capabilities. For example, most states prohibit the purchase of alcoholic beverages

> **FAST FACT**
>
> The United Nations (UN) Convention on the Rights of the Child, ratified in 1989, states:
>
> Article 3: All decisions taken which affect children's lives should be taken in the child's best interest.
>
> Article 12: Children have the right to have their voices heard in all matters concerning them.

by people under age twenty-one, even if their parents consider them mature enough to drink. Whether it makes sense or not, the driving age, the marriage age, and a host of other regulations are based on reaching specific birthdays. Guns are treated in the same way by the national government and most states.

Federal law prohibits gun dealers with a license from selling or delivering shotguns or rifles, or ammunition for shotguns or rifles, to any person whom the dealer knows or believes to be under the age of eighteen. Dealers cannot sell or deliver other firearms, especially handguns, or ammunition for those firearms, to any person whom the dealer knows or believes to be under the age of twenty-one.

Congress has been more lenient regarding firearms sales to children by people without a gun dealer's license. An unlicensed person cannot sell or deliver a handgun or handgun ammunition to any person whom the transferor knows or believes to be under the age of eighteen, but this is three years younger than the restriction on sales by dealers. The law also allows certain exceptions for temporary use by children for specific activities such as ranching, farming, target practice, and hunting. Federal law prohibits, with certain exceptions, the possession of a handgun or handgun ammunition by anyone under the age of eighteen. Congress has specifically refused to pass any age limits for the sale of "long guns," such as hunting rifles or shotguns, by an unlicensed person. Several states have laws similar to the national laws regarding restrictions on gun sales; for example, handgun purchasers must be at least twenty-one, and long gun purchasers must be at least eighteen.

> **FAST FACT**
>
> Illinois is one of the only states with age restrictions that are stricter than those made in Washington, D.C. In Illinois, almost no one under the age of twenty-one may legally purchase or possess a handgun or long gun.

Children and Hunting

Congress's decision to place fewer restrictions on the sale of long guns (as opposed to handguns) reflects a centuries-old American tradition of hunting game for food or recreation. Sport hunting (and, to a lesser degree, target shooting) is one of the only activities in which

children are not only permitted but actually encouraged to use guns. For this reason, federal law sets no minimum age for the possession of rifles or shotguns, which are the types of firearms most commonly used in sport hunting. Although Congress forbids firearms dealers from selling long guns to anyone under the age of eighteen, the law has significant loopholes. In states where there is no state minimum for owning a long gun, a child of any age can legally buy a rifle or shotgun from an unlicensed person.

Hunting animals with guns, especially in the rural South and West, was and remains a basic part of many boys' transition into manhood. (Girls are much less frequently involved in this "hunting culture.") Supporters of hunting claim that it educates young people to respect the intelligence, beauty, and power of animals and is an ideal way to teach generosity, humility, courage, and fortitude. Supporters also emphasize the social aspects of hunting, especially the friendship and mutual

Stephanie Lathrup, nineteen, of Marion, Illinois, is one of 1.2 million female hunters in the United States today, according to the U.S. Fish and Wildlife Service. At present, there are no federal laws prohibiting the use by or the sale to minors of long guns (the type most commonly used in hunting).

encouragement (often known as "male bonding") that boys enjoy on hunting trips with close friends, fathers, uncles, or older brothers. On the other hand, opponents belittle the "manliness" of hunting and criticize the unequal competition between unarmed animals and high-powered firearms. They believe that killing animals for pleasure or symbolic food acquisition or to promote male bonding and tradition is inappropriate and that there are better sources of family values, nature appreciation, exercise, and food than sport hunting.

Regardless of which side is correct in this philosophical debate, hunting seems to be an activity in long-term decline in the United States, especially among young people. Between 1955 and 1980, the percentage of the American population twelve years of age or older that hunted ranged between 9 and 11 percent. Beginning in 1975, the numbers began to decline: 9.9 percent in 1975; 9.1 percent in 1980; 8.4 percent in 1985; and 7.5 percent in 1991. In 1996, according to the U.S. Fish and Wildlife Service, about 13.8 million Americans sixteen and older hunted, representing about 5.3 percent of the total U.S. population. Between 1996 and 2001, that number

In order to promote a declining sport, the sport hunting industry markets the activity to young people. This photograph shows children and adults in a covered wagon waiting to leave for Virginia's Southern Heritage deer hunt. Designed to thin the herds of whitetail deer in Chippokes Plantation State Park, the day's program featured a number of festive events mirroring seventeenth- and eighteenth-century colonial hunting traditions and celebrations.

apparently declined to 13 million. A report by hunting advocates conceded,

> The future for hunting looks bleak given prevailing social values coupled with recent and projected trends in American demographics.... Nearly every published report of hunting trends indicates that the number of participants has declined during the decade of the 1980s and forecasts continued decline into the future.

The immediate reason for the decline is relatively simple; the typical hunter in 2001 was forty-two, white, and male, and the average age for such hunters was increasing. Young hunters are not coming along in sufficient numbers to sustain the sport when older hunters drop out. Increasing suburban sprawl has also had an impact; hunting is most popular in rural areas, but rural areas are fast disappearing. Real estate development pushes wildlife habitat farther and farther away from where most Americans live, making hunting time-consuming and inconvenient for most of the population, especially those with children. The rise in two-career families means that adults have fewer opportunities to hunt, with or without children along. Single-parent households, usually headed by a woman, increased dramatically in the 1980s and 1990s. Mothers rarely introduce their children to hunting and are more likely than fathers to object to their children taking up hunting.

Men and women who do not start hunting by the time they graduate from high school are unlikely ever to start. Nationwide, 54 percent of all hunters began hunting before they turned thirteen, 69 percent began before they turned sixteen, and 83 percent before they turned nineteen. Other nature sports, such as rock climbing, orienteering, caving, and even skiing are regularly taken up for the first time by young adults. Many young people, however, now choose not to hunt because they find killing animals for recreation offensive. A survey by a pro-hunting group in 1997 found that "about 15 percent of U.S. youth [aged thirteen to twenty] are very interested in hunting while over half (52 percent) have no interest at all in hunting. Of the youth who are not interested in hunting, the main reasons given for the lack of interest are 'against killing animals' (52 percent) and 'animals have a right to live' (13 percent)."

Recruiting Children to Hunt

Because the trends leading to the decline of hunting do not seem likely to change in the next few decades, the sport hunting industry, state wildlife agencies, and the U.S. Fish and Wildlife Service are mounting a massive campaign to recruit children into hunting and the usage of firearms. A growing number of states offer inexpensive hunting licenses for children under a certain age, usually sixteen. Colorado's "Youth Combination Small Game Hunting, Furbearer, and Fishing License" costs just one dollar, as opposed to fifteen dollars for an adult license. New Jersey offers resident and nonresident children ages ten through thirteen a hunting license for three dollars, compared to twenty-two dollars for a resident adult license or a hundred dollars for nonresidents.

Although people under age eighteen cannot legally own rifles or shotguns in many states, the firearms industry often encourages parents and other adults to purchase guns for children. Advertisements from gun manufacturers and state wildlife agencies frequently model children using guns. The front cover of *New Jersey's Fish and Game Regulations* for 1998–99 depicted a watercolor of a man and a young boy apparently under the age of ten walking into the woods together. Both are wearing blaze orange vests and carrying shotguns. The hunting regulations included application forms for New Jersey's "Take a Kid Pheasant Hunting" and "Be a Hunting Mentor" programs. The children's pheasant hunting program, which teaches children as young as ten years old how to shoot and kill birds, was partially sponsored by a grant from the National Rifle Association (NRA).

Gun advocacy groups have a particular stake in encouraging children to hunt. The NRA has launched a multimillion-dollar campaign to encourage kids to take up hunting and sport shooting. Former NRA president Marion Hammer declared that the organization is in "an old-fashioned wrestling match for the hearts and minds of our children, and we'd better engage our adversaries with no holds barred." In a monthly column in *Guns & Ammo* magazine, NRA president Charlton Heston encouraged gun owners to "consider how you can help preserve freedom for future Americans by introducing a young person to the fun and satisfaction of shooting.... [Take] your daughter, nephew, neighbor or family friend out for an afternoon of plinking, hunting or clay target excitement." The NRA sponsors year-round shooting camps and hunter education programs for young people and provides a monthly magazine for junior members.

A growing number of private hunting reserves are now offering special family events to promote hunting as a wholesome sport. Stan Hayek (center) runs his family's farm and hunting preserve in Clutier, Iowa, and works as a hunting guide for many of the father-and-son teams who visit.

By the 1999–2000 hunting season, every state in the United States except Alaska was holding a children's hunt. The Florida Game and Fresh Water Fish Commission, which sponsored the first children's hunt in 1985, now provides special hunts on public land for children as young as eight years old. Fourteen states, including Arkansas, Ohio, New Mexico, and Maryland, have children's hunts with no minimum age limit at all. The hunts are held on public land, usually state-owned wildlife management areas or National Forest lands run by the U.S. Department of Agriculture.

In order to give young people a better chance to gain the satisfaction that comes from killing an animal, these hunts usually take place before the start of a regular hunting season or on days when the sites are closed to avoid competition with more experienced adult hunters. State governments support these children's hunts; state wildlife agencies typically plan and manage the hunts; establish the dates, locations, and regulations; issue the licenses; and police the sites. During California's numerous children's pheasant hunts, the birds are released in the direct vicinity of the children to make it easier for them to kill the birds. Colorado and Ohio have set aside specific parcels of land as "youth hunting areas" for the entire hunting season.

Some doubters suggest that most children who participate in these youth hunts would have become hunters anyway. Many state wildlife agencies and gun advocacy groups believe, however, that children's hunts are an excellent way to recruit children into sport hunting and firearms usage.

Easy Access to Guns

Despite the decline of hunting and the fact that the law in most cases prohibits children from using firearms without adult supervision, young people seem to have no difficulty getting guns. Surveys consistently show that more than a third of households in the United States keep firearms in

the home or car, and about 20 percent of these guns are left loaded and unlocked. This means that millions of children live in homes with easily accessible and potentially lethal guns. In October 2000, the U.S. Secret Service released a study of thirty-seven school shootings in twenty-six states. The study concluded that in two-thirds of the cases, the attackers got the guns from their own homes or those of relatives.

Especially in the late 1980s and early 1990s, children's access to guns became a national issue. The firearms homicide rate for ten- to fourteen-year-olds in the United States more than doubled between 1985 and 1992. In a survey of children in grades six through twelve, more than half said that they could get a gun if they wanted to. According to the 2001 report on youth violence by the U.S. Surgeon General, the so-called violence epidemic that occurred between 1983 and 1993 was specifically tied to more young people carrying guns.

Gun shows around the country often draw protests from local area residents interested in shutting them down. Despite efforts to close the Great Western Gun Show in Pomona, California, the show successfully drew thousands of patrons from all over the state.

The number of young people carrying guns declined in the late 1990s and early 2000s. Fortunately, fewer students carried guns in general, and fewer brought guns to school. However, weapons still seem to be readily available; a recent survey of high school students indicated that 61 percent "know someone who brings a gun to school" and that 24 percent of the students believe that they could "easily get a gun if I wanted one."

Curiosity about Guns

Children are often impulsive; they sometimes act without thinking about the outcome. This behavior can have disastrous results when young people come into contact with guns. The easy availability of guns is also a potential problem, because children are naturally curious, especially when it comes to weapons. If a gun can be found in someone's home, there is a good chance that a child will find it and play with it. Almost every child who has picked

Despite efforts to educate children at home and in school about the danger of guns, many young people are still intrigued and seduced by the power of guns. Teenagers Jamie Rouse (right) and Stephen Abbott were charged with two counts of first-degree murder in the shooting deaths of a teacher and a student, casualties of the "violence epidemic" that has claimed the lives of many of the nation's young people.

up a gun and shot someone, accidentally or not, was told not to play with guns. Talking to children about the dangers of firearms is rarely sufficient.

This point was driven home in a fascinating study in the medical journal *Pediatrics*. Eight- to twelve-year-old boys were recruited from families that completed a survey on firearms ownership, storage practices, and parental beliefs. Small groups of three boys were then placed in a room with a one-way mirror and observed for up to fifteen minutes. Two water pistols and an actual .380-caliber handgun were hidden in separate drawers. The handgun contained a radio transmitter that activated a light whenever the trigger was pressed with enough force to fire the gun. Twenty-nine groups of boys took part in the study; twenty-one of the groups discovered the handgun, and sixteen groups handled it. One or more boys in ten of the groups pulled the trigger with enough force to fire the gun. After the exercise, about half of the forty-eight boys who had handled the gun stated that they either thought that it was a toy or were unsure whether it was real. Parents' beliefs about their children's interest in guns had no effect on the actual behavior of the boys when they found the handgun. Boys who were believed to have a low interest in real guns were just as likely to handle the gun or pull the trigger as boys who were thought to have a high interest in guns. More than 90 percent of the boys who handled the gun or pulled the trigger reported that they had previously received some sort of gun-safety instruction.

The producers of a television news show performed a similar study with older boys in 2000. They placed a disabled gun in a room and then observed the response of more than fifty teenagers when they found it. Many of the boys, including those who had recently received warnings to stay away from guns, played with the gun, checked the chambers, loaded ammunition clips, or even aimed it at other teenagers. The experiment confirmed that even young men who claimed that they would stay away from firearms were so seduced by the sight of a gun that they could not resist the urge to touch it and play with it.

This is not to say that educating kids about the danger of guns is useless, but warnings seem to have little effect on their behavior in the presence of an actual gun. Some of the thirteen- to eighteen-year-old boys who took part in the experiment seemed to change when they found the gun; some became secretive and put on gloves so as not to leave fingerprints. The researcher for the program concluded, "What else do you do with a gun? You shoot someone.... [Teenage boys'] egocentricity and needing to be in the spotlight, plus their recklessness and sense of invulnerability, is going to lead them to engage in dangerous behaviors with a weapon."

Placing the Responsibility on Kids

Although children are naturally curious about guns, parents often reassure themselves by adopting beliefs that relieve them of much of the responsibility of having a gun in the home. Instead, adults tend to place the burden on children to protect themselves from the misuse of guns. One study in 2003 said that the vast majority of American adults believe their children would not touch guns that they found. More than half of the people in the study explained that their children were "too smart" or "knew better" than to handle guns. Less than half based their predictions on specific instructions that they had given their children. Only 12 percent of these owners (15 out of 122) stored guns locked and unloaded, although a similar study reported that nearly 50 percent of gun owners who were parents of four- to twelve-year-olds stored their guns locked and unloaded.

Most parents have unrealistic ideas about their children's developmental levels and impulse control. This explains why so many parents and child-care providers fail to store guns safely or even discuss gun-safety issues with children. Even if parents have spoken to their children about guns, the discussion will probably not stop a child

> **FAST FACT**
>
> In one study, three-fourths of gun-owning parents believed that their four- to twelve-year-old children could tell the difference between a toy gun and a real gun. Almost one-fourth believed that their children could be trusted with loaded firearms.

from handling a gun. The director of the Injury Prevention Program at Children's Hospital in Boston notes that "any small child who picks up a gun...is going to put a finger on the trigger and click it."

The Symbolic Power of Guns for Children

Almost by definition, children under the age of eighteen have no power. They lack any meaningful economic resources, and adult law constantly imposes itself on their lives—for example, forcing them to go to school. The fact that guns—especially handguns—are forbidden to children makes them a symbol of adulthood. As in the case of alcohol, cigarettes, and sex, minors are naturally drawn to participate in those activities that seem to define being an adult in the United States in the twenty-first century.

Firearms are also a symbol of power, especially for boys. Possession of a gun makes a dangerous force out of

Fourteen-year-old Josh Brady testifies before a Senate committee in Indianapolis in 1996. The committee was considering a bill making it an infraction for adults to store a loaded handgun where children could have access to it. Brady's friend had been accidentally shot and killed by another boy who was curious about a handgun he found at home.

even the weakest twelve-year-old. This fact hasn't changed since Samuel Colt's first handgun marketing campaign before the Civil War (1861–1865): "God may have made men, but Samuel Colt made them equal." Through movies, television, video games, and compact discs, boys learn to closely tie male authority, and even being a man, to the ability to fire a gun. One researcher commented, "From the time kids are big enough to pick them up, for the rest of their lives, they're just fascinated with [guns]."

This fascination with guns seems to be primarily male. Traditional views of manhood in the United States encourage men to seek success, status, and control; men should be tough and self-reliant, take risks, and be aggressive. The possession and use of a gun easily plays into these stereotypes. Young boys, seeking to achieve manhood in a changing American society without any real rites of initiation, find in guns a symbolic answer to many of their questions about power, prestige, and authority.

Child Access Prevention Laws

In 1997, 142 children aged fourteen and under died from accidental gunshot wounds, and 127 more were firearms suicides. In the mid-1990s, the rate of unintentional firearms-related deaths for children under age fifteen was nine times greater in the United States than in twenty-five other industrialized countries combined. Yet a 1999 survey found that 30 percent of gun owners in households with children under the age of eighteen reported that they stored guns either loaded or both loaded and unlocked.

Because many gun owners feel that locking a gun up (especially a handgun) or storing it unloaded would make it next to useless for self-defense, it is difficult to encourage safe storage practices. Although many parents do not understand that curious children cannot always be trusted around weapons, many state laws assign parents this responsibility, whether they like it or not. These states have passed child access prevention (CAP) laws, which punish adults who leave firearms accessible to children. In some states, gun dealers must provide purchasers with a written warning about the law and place a warning sign at the counter. In this way, CAP laws raise public awareness of the problem of unintended gun use and provide a reasonable solution.

There are no federal CAP laws, but as of 2002, nearly twenty individual states had passed CAP laws. Florida passed the first one in 1989. These state CAP laws vary in several important respects. Connecticut's law applies only when a person is killed as a result of the unsafe storage practice. On the other hand, a parent or owner in Hawaii is liable the moment that a child gains access to a gun that is not stored safely. California takes a middle position: a gun owner who stores a weapon improperly is guilty when a child uses a gun to kill, injure, or threaten a third person or carries the weapon in a public place. The majority of state CAP laws apply only when a gun is loaded, even if ammunition is stored nearby. However, a few states, such as Hawaii, also impose liability when a gun is unloaded.

Child access prevention (CAP) bills are gaining in popularity around the country. Illinois governor George Ryan signed his state's CAP law in 1999. Gun owners in Illinois now face fines or jail time if children under fourteen hurt someone with carelessly stored firearms.

The age of the children covered by the CAP law also varies from state to state. Most state laws apply to children under the age of sixteen. Virginia's CAP law applies to children under the age of fourteen (and in some cases, under the age of twelve). North Carolina and Delaware have much stricter laws, holding gun owners responsible if unsafe storage leads to any child under the age of eighteen gaining access to a gun.

The Effectiveness of CAP Laws

The definition of "safe storage," like the term "children," is open to a variety of interpretations. Most CAP laws do not define "safe storage" and do not require gun owners to store their firearms in any specific way. Instead, they simply impose liability on an adult when a child gains access to an improperly stored firearm. They usually do not apply if the gun is kept in a locked container or otherwise can't be operated. Massachusetts has a general

This photograph illustrates a gun-disabling trigger lock, a device intended to be used on all stored firearms, thus preventing children from pulling the trigger.

locking device law (that does not specifically mention children or child safety), making it unlawful for a person to keep any firearm unless it is stored in a locked container or equipped with an effective safety device that is in use at the time.

In states that have enacted CAP laws, firearms-related deaths of children, and especially accidental deaths, seem to have decreased within two years after the laws went into effect. A 1997 study of twelve states with CAP or safe storage laws found that after these laws went into effect, unintentional firearms deaths among children under the age of fifteen fell 23 percent. A 2000 study that reexamined the same question suggested that CAP laws vary widely in their effectiveness. In particular, Florida's success may be unique. It was the first state to pass a CAP law; its law allows for the harshest penalties for violators (one of only three CAP laws that allows for felony prosecution of violators); and the state had an unusually high rate of unintentional firearms deaths among young people before the law passed.

Where Children, Guns, and the Law Meet

Although crime by children and young adults carrying guns declined from 1993 to 2003, American gun violence involving youth still remains at levels that most people find troubling. CAP laws punish adults when children gain access to improperly stored guns, but what of the responsibility of children themselves? In many cases, violations of gun laws by underage youths do not seem to be handled well in the regular criminal justice system. Juvenile and family courts have often been criticized for punishing young offenders involved in gun crimes either too much or too little and for failing to provide appropriate counseling and educational services.

The juvenile gun court, a new, experimental type of specialty court, deals with young people who have committed a gun crime that has not resulted in serious physical injury. Most juvenile gun courts are short-term programs that do not replace normal juvenile courts, but instead work with them. These new gun courts, modeled after successful youth drug court programs, try to use small caseloads, frequent hearings, immediate punishments, family involvement, and a variety of educational and psychological counseling services in order to break the connection between youthful offenders and firearms. It remains to be seen whether this new type of court will be more effective in controlling gun violence than more traditional methods. As in other instances where gun use and ownership intersect with the law, juvenile gun courts attempt to compromise between the potential seriousness of the misuse of guns and the unintentional recklessness and bravado of young people.

CHAPTER 2

Youth Homicide, Suicide, and Firearms Accidents

The debate over protecting children from gun violence took on added significance after the 1960s when the firearms-related homicide rate for children, both as victims and as killers, began to rise. From 1950 to 1993, the overall annual death rate for American children aged less than fifteen years greatly decreased. The number of young people who died from unintentional injuries, pneumonia, influenza, cancer, polio, and birth defects declined considerably in those years. During the same period, however, childhood homicide rates tripled and suicide rates quadrupled. By 1994, homicide was the third-leading cause of death and suicide the sixth-leading cause among children aged five to fourteen years. Much of this increased violence involved children with guns.

This increase in youth violence was particularly large in the 1970s and 1980s. To a certain degree, this reflected the rising crime rate for all age groups in the United States. The homicide rate for all Americans doubled from the mid-1960s to the late 1970s. In 1980, it peaked at 10.2 per 100,000 people and subsequently fell off to 7.9 per 100,000 in 1985. It rose again in the late 1980s and early 1990s to another peak in 1991 of 9.8 per 100,000.

However, both the rising crime and homicide rates were driven by offenses by young people aged fourteen to twenty-four. In fact, the rate at which teenagers and young adults became victims of murder increased dramatically in the late 1980s, while rates for older age groups actually declined. The homicide victimization rate for those aged fourteen to seventeen increased almost 150 percent between 1985 and 1993. The rates at which teenagers and young adults committed murder followed a similar pattern, increasing dramatically in the late 1980s, while rates for older age groups declined. The homicide offense rates of fourteen- to seventeen-year-olds exploded after 1985, exceeding even the rates of twenty-five- to thirty-four-year-olds and thirty-five- to forty-nine-year-olds.

Decrease in Youth Violence in the 1990s

Beginning in the early 1990s, the crime rate began to decrease for all ages. By 2003, homicide rates had dropped to levels last seen in the late 1960s. Rates for violent crimes, which include rape, robbery, aggravated assault, and homicide, have also declined for all age groups since 1993. In 2001, violent crime rates reached the lowest level ever recorded by the National Crime Victimization Survey, although they remained higher than in most other industrialized nations. The homicide rate for all Americans dropped to 6.3 per 100,000 in 1998, 5.7 in 1999, 5.5 in 2000, and then rose slightly to 5.6 in 2001.

Older teens and young adults still are the most likely people to murder someone else and to be murdered. Since 1993, victimization rates for older teens and young adults have declined but remain higher than the levels of the mid-1980s. At the same time, the victimization rates for males aged fourteen to seventeen declined to levels lower than those for people age twenty-five and older. In the

Despite the decrease in youth violence since 1990, schools around the country continue to be vigilant in their violence-prevention programs. In this photograph, police in Birmingham, Alabama, use metal detectors to search band members, fans, and players in an attempt to prevent the possible outbreak of violence during a high school football game.

early 2000s, the victimization rate for children aged fourteen to seventeen has declined to levels that are approximately the same as they were from 1976 to 1985.

The reasons for the decline in youth violence, like the reasons for its rise, are numerous, varied, and greatly disputed. Public officials and politicians boast that increased numbers of police and tougher sentencing of criminals have led to the decline. Gun control supporters point to restrictions on firearms, such as the Brady Handgun Violence Protection Act of 1993, which prevents criminals from gaining easy access to guns. Gun advocacy groups cite the loosening of gun control laws on the state level, such as the increased acceptance of concealed-carry laws. Economists point to an improved job market for most of the 1990s; social scientists note the declining percentage of teenagers compared to the rest of the population, due to a falling birthrate in the 1980s and greater life expectancy, as well as the stabilization of the crack cocaine drug trade in the cities. Whatever the main reason or reasons, the results are dramatic.

For example, in 2002, there were only eighty-two murders in the borough of Manhattan in New York City. This was fewer than in any other year since the end of the 1800s; at no time in the entire 1900s were there ever less than 100 murders in Manhattan. The peak year was 1972, when there were 661 homicides in Manhattan, but as recently as 1990, there were 590 murders there. In 2002, all of New York City, the nation's most populous city, recorded only 590 murders. In contrast, Los Angeles, California, with approximately half the population of New York City, totaled 654 homicides. The difference is commonly explained by increased gang violence in California.

Gangs and Guns

Since the 1970s, there has been a dramatic increase in gang activity in the United States. In the 1970s, gangs were active in less than half the states, but now every state reports at least some youth gang activity. The number of

cities reporting youth gang problems increased from fewer than 300 in the 1970s to more than 2,500 in 1998. Like the crime rate, the overall number of gangs and gang members in the United States has decreased slightly since 1996. However, in medium- and large-sized cities, gang involvement remains near peak levels. In 2000, about 24,000 different youth gangs around the country enrolled more than 700,000 adolescents and young adults as gang members. Most gang members are between the ages of twelve and twenty-four; the average age is about seventeen. Gang membership is a brief phase for most young people. Three studies that tracked teenagers over time found that more than one-half of youth gang members leave the gang within their first year of membership.

Unfortunately, youth gang violence with guns has increased dramatically over the past thirty years. Most gang members are already involved in illegal activities, often including violence, before they join gangs. Gangs

In 1990, gang violence had reached epic proportions, forcing local gang leaders to impose their own cease-fires. Here, the cofounder of the Los Angeles Crips gang, Mike Concepcion (seated), along with rap singer Tone Loc (right), calls for a gang truce in a housing project in the crime-ridden Watts section of Los Angeles.

recruit or attract these potentially or already violent individuals; many already own and carry guns. Involvement in violent activities increases during periods of gang membership and usually decreases after members leave the gang. Gang members are much more likely than other young people to commit serious and violent crimes. For example, a survey in Denver, Colorado, found that while less than one-fifth of city youth were gang members, they were responsible for committing more than four-fifths of the serious violent crimes. Youth gang homicides, often committed with firearms, seem to result more from conflict between gangs than from the drug trade. Researchers believe that gang violence has become much more dangerous because of the use of cars in drive-by attacks on other gangs and the increasing availability of more lethal weapons.

Handguns and Youth Violence

Guns, especially handguns, seem to have played a major role in both the rise of the crime rate in the 1970s and 1980s and its decline in the 1990s. From 1970 to 2000, the

In October 2000, the volunteer group City Year set 3,792 pairs of shoes on the front steps of Trinity Church in Boston, representing the number of people under nineteen years of age who are killed annually in the United States by handguns.

trend in homicides that did not involve firearms showed almost no change. On the other hand, homicides committed with handguns by teens and young adults rose sharply beginning in the mid-1980s, making up almost the entire growth in homicides in the period from 1985 to 1993. The sharp increase in homicides in the late 1980s can be directly attributed to handgun violence by teenagers and young adults, especially young males under age twenty. Likewise, the more recent sharp decrease in handgun homicides and gun crimes by teenagers is an important factor in the overall decline in the crime and murder rate since the early 1990s. Nonetheless, of the approximately 1,400 juveniles murdered in 2001, 44 percent were killed with firearms.

In the mid-1980s, not only did handguns replace fists and knives as common weapons for settling disputes among young people, but there was a sharp growth in the use of handguns by teenagers to commit robberies, as well as homicides. That rise in firearms homicides changed what had been a stable trend in homicides committed by young people to a sharply rising one with the greatest increases for children aged eighteen and under. There was no similar growth in homicides committed with other guns (such as rifles) or nongun weapons. This suggests (although it is, of course, disputed) that the use of handguns, rather than an increase in violent attitudes among young people, was one of the most important reasons for the increase in violent crime in the late 1980s and early 1990s. In fact, nongun homicides among all age groups declined steadily from 1985 to 1997.

> **FAST FACT**
>
> In comparison to the youth record, there was a downward trend in adult homicides by all weapons, especially by handguns. Overall, there has been little change over the years in the mix of weapons used by adults in homicides.

Teenagers Carrying Guns

It's almost certain that in the late 1980s and early 1990s, an increasing number of young people carried handguns and that this increase fueled a rise in youth homicide rates. Even though federal law prohibits the sale of handguns to people under age twenty-one and possession of handguns by juveniles, it is apparently not difficult for young people to gain access to guns or even carry them. Some national surveys have reported that almost 10 percent of male high school students carried a gun in the thirty days before being surveyed. Gun carrying is even more common in high-crime areas, where 25 percent of male teenagers carry guns, and among high-risk groups more than 80 percent of male juvenile offenders report having carried a gun. Somewhere between 40,000 and 200,000 students in grades six to twelve carry firearms to school at least once in a school year, out of approximately 23 million students in these grades.

Young people who carry guns claim that their major reason for possessing a weapon is concern for their own safety. In one national survey, 43 percent of high school students who admitted carrying a gun within the past year claimed that they carried it primarily for protection. The problem, of course, is that when an argument breaks out, teenagers who carry guns may use them immediately, especially if they think that their adversaries also have guns.

The arrest rate for weapons charges is one possible, if imperfect, indicator of how frequently teenagers carry guns. For the years from 1975 to 2000, the rates of arrest for weapon possession for young people ages eighteen and under show a remarkable similarity to the homicide patterns for the same ages. The weapons arrest trends for youth show a relatively flat period of slight growth until about 1985, a sharp rise peaking in 1993, and then a clear decline.

Of course, it's possible that increases or decreases in weapons arrests might not result from increases or decreases in illegal firearms, but only changes in the energy that police expend in searching for illegal guns. One group of researchers, however, found that one of the major reasons that delinquent adolescents decide not to carry a gun is the fear of being arrested. This research suggested that aggressive stop-and-frisk tactics by local police, the growth of community groups that negotiated

FAST FACT

Some gun advocates claim that there is little evidence that teenagers carried weapons more frequently in the 1980s, other than the increase in gun violence. Instead, they blame the huge increase in teenage firearms fatalities on drug and gang wars.

Young people who carry guns for safety purposes may put themselves and others at great risk when they solve difficult problems or defuse volatile situations with violence. Brenda Spencer (pictured) was convicted of killing two students at her San Diego high school in 1979 when she used a gun in response to emotional problems she had.

truces among gangs, and attempts to establish community norms against gun carrying all helped reduce the rates of teenagers carrying guns. This decrease may have had a ripple effect; as a result, other young people felt less need to carry guns for self-protection, which may have been a factor in the decrease in homicide and robbery by youth in the mid- to late 1990s.

Children as Killers

In general, murders by teens involve guns. Homicides by teens and young adults are much more likely to be committed with guns than homicides by people of other ages. The following chart not only shows how deeply guns are involved in murders by young people but also gives a sense of the huge increase in youth violence in the late 1980s and its general decline in the 1990s.

Homicides by Weapon and Age of Offender

YEAR	UNDER AGE 14		AGE 14 TO 17	
	GUN	NONGUN	GUN	NONGUN
1980	59	53	1,185	898
1985	54	39	855	581
1990	58	45	2,325	817
1995	98	40	2,692	741
2000	36	33	1,084	408

In 1995, a Boston group called Stop Handgun Violence placed 200 posters around the state of Massachusetts featuring pictures of children who were killed by guns.

Source: U.S. Department of Justice

Young People as Victims

In 1997, people aged twelve to twenty-four made up 22 percent of the total U.S. population, but 35 percent of all murder victims and 49 percent of all serious violent crime victims. Most killers of young people use guns, so it's not surprising that the majority of young homicide victims have died as a result of being shot.

The percentage of homicide victims killed with guns increases with age up to age seventeen and then begins a long, gradual decline. Not until age sixty-three, however, does the number of nongun homicides finally surpass the number of murders committed with guns.

Percent of Homicides Involving Guns by Victims' Age

AGE OF VICTIM	GUN	NONGUN
5	28 percent	72 percent
8	37 percent	63 percent
11	49 percent	51 percent
14	69 percent	31 percent
17	77 percent	23 percent
20	74 percent	26 percent
23	73 percent	27 percent
26	71 percent	29 percent
29	69 percent	31 percent
32	68 percent	32 percent

Source: U.S. Department of Justice

Self-Defense by Children

Although people under age twenty-one cannot generally own handguns, and although most states forbid children under age eighteen from owning rifles or shotguns, the firearms industry and gun advocacy groups often encourage gun use by children and encourage parents and other adults to purchase guns for them. Advertisements from gun manufacturers frequently model children using guns. The National Shooting Sports Foundation (NSSF) promotional materials claim that any child old enough to be left alone in the house for two or three hours or sent to the grocery store with a list and a twenty-dollar bill is old enough to own a gun.

In an article titled "Loaded Guns Can Be Good for Kids," two law school professors argue that children should not be prevented from using handguns for self-defense. They conclude that "if a family must live in a dangerous neighborhood, and if the parents have taught gun safety to responsible older children, then having the gun ready for immediate protection might be safer. Parents, not members of Congress, are best suited to make these kinds of decisions."

Comparison with Other Countries

The United States has long had a reputation for violence. This is somewhat misleading, because the nation has avoided the ethnic and religious conflicts that have torn apart many places in the world. The U.S. Civil War took place more than 140 years ago, and the rule of law generally prevails in most places in the country. Nonetheless, for reasons that are endlessly debated, the homicide rate in the United States does not compare well to that of other industrialized nations, and this is especially true for homicides of American children.

In 1996, just after the height of the wave of youth crime and violence in the 1990s, the Centers for Disease Control (CDC) compared general patterns of homicide, suicide, and firearms-related death in the United States and twenty-five other industrialized countries. The CDC used a sample of 161 million children under fifteen; 57 million (35 percent) were in the United States and 104 million (65 percent) were in the other twenty-five countries.

The report concluded the United States has the highest rates of childhood homicide, suicide, and firearms-related death among industrialized countries. Compared with children in the other nations, American children under fifteen were twelve times more likely to die from gunfire, sixteen times more likely to be murdered by a gun, eleven times more likely to commit suicide with a gun, and nine times more likely to die in a firearms accident. In general, 73 percent of all murders of children under fifteen occurred among Americans. The total homicide rate for children in the United States was five times higher than that for children in the other twenty-five countries combined. (The nonfirearms-related homicide rate in the United States was also nearly four times the rate of all the other countries combined.) Not surprisingly, one of the greatest worries of ten- to seventeen-year-olds in America was violent crime.

The rate of firearms-related deaths among children in the United States was more than twice as high as that in Finland, the country with the next-highest rate. However, among the other nations, the impact of firearms-related deaths varied a great deal. Firearms were the primary cause of homicide in Finland, Israel, Australia, Italy, Germany, England, and Wales. The sharp decrease in the American homicide rate since 1996 has undoubtedly reduced the divide between the firearms-related death rate among children in the United States and those in the rest of the industrialized world.

Protesters in Denver, Colorado, in 1999 gather on the capitol steps to protest legislation that would eliminate local gun control laws across the state.

Suicide

Many Americans think about committing suicide at some time in their lives. Most people, however, do not kill themselves; they come to understand that although the crisis may or may not be temporary, death is permanent and inescapable. When children commit suicide, it's particularly tragic, since children are more likely than adults to respond to an impulse and less likely to understand the results of their actions.

Unfortunately, youth suicide is not rare. It doesn't seem right when a teenager who has lived for such a short time chooses to die, but adolescents who can't get over their depression sometimes do kill themselves. In 2000, suicide was the third-most common cause of death among people aged fifteen to twenty-four; 1,928 Americans nineteen years old or younger committed suicide; 1,007 of them used firearms to kill themselves. The same year, 490 children fifteen years old or younger committed suicide; 206 of these tragedies involved firearms.

Almost half of all teenage suicides involve handguns, a fact that gun control advocates believe illustrates the need for stricter controls. This photograph shows Jake Novak, a high school senior in Kirkwood, Missouri, who launched a group he called Students Working Against Depression.

In the past twenty-five years, suicide in the United States has decreased, but the rate for young people between ages fifteen and twenty-four has tripled. Suicide rates for fifteen- to nineteen-year-olds increased about 11 percent between 1981 and 1997, but suicide rates for those between the ages of ten and fourteen increased an astonishing 80 percent in the same period. Both age groups have shown small declines in recent years.

Guns and Suicide in the United States

In 2000, more than 29,000 Americans committed suicide—a rate of 10.66 suicides per 100,000 people. This average put the United States roughly in the middle of industrialized nations—it was a higher rate than in the United Kingdom, Spain, and Canada, but lower than in Germany, Sweden, and France. Because the U.S. homicide rate declined so sharply after 1993, the number of Americans who commit suicide with guns each year now surpasses those who are killed by others with firearms. In 2000, government statistics revealed that 16,586 suicides were committed using firearms; in contrast, there were 10,801 homicides using guns. These statistics are focusing new attention on suicide, a subject that has long been taboo for many Americans. The tragic toll of suicide, partly hidden from view by the violent crime wave of the 1980s, has now become a topic of concern and debate.

In 2000, 57 percent of suicides were committed using firearms; 14,454 were committed by men and 2,132 by women. Men are much more likely to use guns in suicide attempts; in 2000, 61 percent of all male suicides were committed using a gun, compared with 37 percent of all female suicides. In addition, a gun was the most common weapon used in suicides by senior citizens; 72 percent of suicides committed by the elderly involved firearms.

The purchase of a handgun is related to an increased risk of suicide for at least six years. Many people who intend to commit suicide buy a handgun just for that purpose; in the first week after the purchase of a handgun, the rate of suicide by means of firearms among purchasers was fifty-seven times higher than the suicide rate of the general population. Furthermore, in the first year after buying a handgun, suicide was still the leading cause of death among purchasers, accounting for about a quarter of all deaths. Another study compared the suicide rate in different regions of the United States based on levels of handgun ownership. The researchers concluded that regions with higher levels of household handgun ownership have higher rates of firearms suicide, lower rates of nonfirearms suicide, and higher levels of overall suicide. This relationship cannot be explained, even when taking into account regional differences in mental health indicators, such as lifetime rates of major depression or suicidal thoughts.

Nonetheless, there is reason to think, based on the high nongun suicide rates in other countries, that an adult who wants to commit suicide will do so, whether or not he or she has a gun available. Gun-related suicide rates in the United States may be at world-record levels, but a suicide is just as much a tragedy by whatever means it is committed. It's not clear whether decreasing or controlling gun ownership would have any effect on total suicide rates in the United States or simply shift some suicides from guns to other types of weapons. High suicide levels are unfortunate but may not be linked to American gun ownership, especially given the high suicide levels elsewhere.

FAST FACT

In 2000, there were approximately twelve suicides for every 100,000 young people aged twenty to twenty-four and eight suicides for every 100,000 teenagers aged fifteen to nineteen.

Suicide and Young People

The role of firearms in the suicide of young people, however, may differ from their role in adult suicide. Adults may simply switch to another method if a gun is not available for a suicide attempt. By 1990, handguns were the method of choice in nearly 70 percent of suicides by teenagers aged fifteen to nineteen—up 20 percent since 1970. The increase in the rate of youth suicide (and the number of deaths by suicide) over the

past forty years seems to be largely related to the use of firearms as a method.

In 1996, in Jasper County, South Carolina, two teenagers are found shot to death on Interstate 95, possible victims of a murder-suicide.

Because of the internal nature of depression and loneliness, thousands of young people who appear to be happy are actually in deep emotional pain. Although boys commit suicide far more often than girls, no one is immune. In a recent survey of high school students, 60 percent said that they had thought about killing themselves at one time or another. About 9 percent said that they had tried at least once. Another study by the CDC found that one out of eleven college students considered suicide, and the number was higher among people of the same age as college students who were not in college.

There are several different theories about why the youth suicide rate has increased in recent years. The competitive nature of modern American life seems to generate many pressures that increasingly fall upon young people. The competition for good grades and future economic success is stressful. Increased depictions of violence on television and in the newspaper seem to justify violent solutions to problems. Perhaps some parents are not as involved or interested in their children's lives as they could be. Many people have noted a link between the accessibility of guns and youth suicide; it may be easier for kids to get the tools for successful suicide attempts than in previous decades.

The Role of Guns in Adolescent Suicide

Firearms are the most common method of suicide by American youth, regardless of race and gender. Young people in the United States use guns in more than half of all successful suicides. In 2000, 13 percent of all suicides were committed by people under the age of twenty-five; 52 percent of Americans nineteen years old or younger used a gun to commit suicide, while 42 percent of those fifteen and younger used firearms to kill themselves. In general, research has shown that the access to and availability of firearms is a factor in the increase in youth suicide.

Gender is also a factor in firearms-related suicide. School-aged girls may make as many as three times more suicide attempts as boys. Many of these girls' attempts, however, are not extremely lethal or highly dangerous in a medical sense; most of them are drug overdoses or mild wrist cutting. The most common suicidal deaths among minors are teenage boys who die of self-inflicted gunshot wounds.

It's theoretically possible that no youth suicide could be prevented. Nonetheless, suicidal impulses, especially in children, are often fleeting. Many suicides involving a gun might be prevented if a less lethal method were used. Unlike overdosing on pills, there is rarely a second chance when teenagers shoot themselves. When a gun is used in a suicide attempt, a fatal outcome results more than three-quarters of the time.

Younger and Older Teens

Depression, substance abuse, and behavioral problems are more common in teens aged sixteen and older, compared to younger teens. Historically, this puts older teens at higher risk for suicide than younger teens. However, suicide rates are now rising for younger adolescents, as well, with dramatic increases for Americans under sixteen from 1980 to 2000. Each year from 1996 to 2000, an average of 115 children under fifteen years old committed suicide with firearms and at least another 131 died from accidental gunshot wounds. In that same period, more than 5,000 adolescents between fifteen and nineteen years

James Dale Nesbitt, sixteen, of North Providence, Rhode Island, is buried after fatally shooting himself in the head with his father's gun. Police categorized the shooting as an accident.

old killed themselves with firearms and almost 800 more died from accidental gunshot wounds.

The Harvard Injury Control Research Center investigated whether the availability of guns contributed to more than 6,000 child suicides between 1988 and 1997. The study concluded that twice as many suicides are committed by kids between the ages of five and fourteen in the five states where people own the highest number of firearms per capita (Louisiana, Alabama, Mississippi, Arkansas, and West Virginia) than in the five states with the lowest gun ownership (Hawaii, Massachusetts, Rhode Island, New Jersey, and Delaware). Childhood suicides from causes other than guns are roughly similar in both groups of states, but states with high gun ownership had seven times the child gun suicide rate. The study hypothesized that gun availability accounted for the difference. The National Rifle Association (NRA) called the study "trivial" and attacked the results on the grounds that it was impossible to actually determine the number or percentage of Americans who own firearms in any state. The NRA also mentioned that the study examined an extremely small number of the total gun-related deaths in the United States and that the study didn't control for demographic or cultural factors.

Safe Storage of Firearms

The risk of suicide seems to increase dramatically when children and teenagers have access to firearms, particularly loaded guns, at home. One study showed that even among adolescents with no apparent psychiatric disorders or any other suicidal risk factors, loaded household firearms seem to be associated with a higher risk of suicide (although this study didn't control for other possible factors that might have led to suicidal behavior).

Perhaps firearms create a greater risk of suicide because the most common location for the occurrence of firearms suicides by young people is in their own homes. Almost three out of every four guns used in childhood and

adolescent suicide attempts are stored in the homes of the victims or in the homes of relatives or friends. A home with a handgun is more likely to have a teen suicide than a home without a handgun. Nonetheless, one study showed that when parents of depressed, suicide-prone teenagers were advised to remove guns from their homes, only a quarter actually did so.

The NRA, the American Academy of Pediatrics (AAP), and other concerned groups agree that guns should be stored in a way that limits access by children. Most gun owners agree with certain general safety principles. Firearms in a home should be unloaded, locked, and kept out of the reach of children and adolescents. Ammunition should be stored and locked apart from the gun, and the keys for both should be kept separate from other household keys. All keys to any firearms should be kept out of the reach of children and adolescents. There's some

SAFE Colorado, a gun control group, assembles on the steps of the capitol in Denver. John Head, copresident of SAFE, urges voters to support laws that will require safe storage of guns and ban the sale of handguns to those under twenty-one.

It is easy to understand how commonplace accidental shootings are when guns are left available for any curious child to discover while rummaging through household items, such as this jewelery box left out in the open.

evidence that policies that restrict access to handguns are associated with a reduction of firearms suicide by young people.

Accidental Shootings Involving Children

Accidental shooting deaths are tragic but not particularly common; unintentional firearms deaths are a nearly negligible proportion of overall gun deaths, although they may be underreported. In 2000, there were 776 recorded accidental firearms fatalities, or less than 1 percent of the general American accidental death rate. Although teenagers and children are involved in several thousand accidental shootings each year, only 193 children and adolescents under age twenty were accidentally killed by firearms in 2000, and only 86 under age fifteen. These numbers have declined since the mid-1990s.

A study of handgun accidents that involved children sixteen or younger found that the typical accident occurred in the afternoon in the summer when no adult was present. About half took place in the victim's own home and another third in a friend's home. In almost half of the cases, children found the guns in the parents' bedrooms; in a study of eighty-eight fatal gun accidents in California where the victim was under fifteen, almost half of the victims found guns that were kept loaded and unlocked. CAP laws—designed to encourage safe storage by holding gun owners responsible for how their guns are stored in the event that a child is injured with a firearm—seem to slightly decrease the rate of accidental firearms deaths.

Although the image of a toddler coming across a gun in a home or an apartment and killing himself or herself is particularly powerful, only nineteen children under age four were reported as accidental firearms deaths in 2000. Accidental shootings of children under age ten are unusual but not unknown. On December 21, 2001, four-year-old Eli Williams was accidentally shot and killed in his home in Laurel, Maryland, by his six-year-old cousin. The children had been left with an eleven-year-old niece while their mother went Christmas shopping. They found a loaded .357-caliber handgun under the bed belonging to Eli's father, who worked for the U.S. Marine Corps. The children were playing with the weapon when it went off, hitting Eli in the head and killing him instantly.

> **FAST FACT**
>
> Most fatal gun accidents occur not in urban areas but in small towns and rural areas; most involve adolescents and adults.

Statistics

The meaning of the numbers and statistics presented in this chapter often depends on the beliefs and intentions of those who interpret them. Because gun ownership and gun control are such controversial topics in the United States, politics and personal points of view color almost all analysis. Questions such as whether a seventeen-year-old is a child, how a suicide could be prevented, and what level of youth homicide is acceptable are problems that individual readers must decide for themselves.

CHAPTER 3

Guns and Schools

According to American law, young people are required to get an education. This usually means attending a school, which means that children must go away from home to receive their formal education, under the direction of teachers not related personally to the students. Schools can sometimes be chaotic, filled with large numbers of children of a variety of ages supervised by adults who may not know them, care about them, or even live in the neighborhood. Although students are generally safer within the school walls than outside them, the problems of society as a whole do not simply cease to exist when students enter a school.

In surveys taken in 1993, 1995, 1997, and 1999, about 7 percent of high school students reported being threatened or injured with a weapon such as a gun or knife on school property in the previous twelve months. In 1999, about 7 percent of students reported carrying a weapon such as a gun or knife on school property in the past thirty days. That same year, students were victims of about 2.5 million reported crimes at school: 1.6 million thefts and 880,000 nonfatal violent crimes, including more than 180,000 serious violent crimes, such as rape, sexual assault, robbery, and aggravated assault. In comparison, students were victims of 2.1 million crimes away from school: 1 million thefts and 1.1 million nonfatal violent crimes, including 476,000 serious violent crimes. Like the youth homicide rate, the victimization rates at school declined from 1992 to 1999.

Although most schools are fairly free of violence, some—especially in urban areas—experience very high rates of violence. The percentage of students who claim that they have been the victims of violence or the threat of violence in schools more than doubled between 1989 and 2000, and this number is almost certainly understated. A series of multiple-victim shooting incidents in suburban and rural schools in the 1990s tremendously increased Americans' concern about violence in schools. Such shootings have come to be referred to as "rampage"

shootings. (A *rampage* is a course of violent, frenzied behavior or action.) Adults commit similar crimes including rampage shootings at work and in public spaces. However, violent incidents in school upset parents and receive media attention because they involve children in what is ideally supposed to be a setting that is free of violence.

Schools are, in fact, relatively safe havens when it comes to homicide. As a proportion of the whole, very few teenagers carry guns in schools. A far larger percentage of gun violence takes place off school grounds. Yet because guns are the weapon of choice in multiple-victim school shootings, and because these shootings are heavily reported in the news media, the relationship between children and firearms has become one of the focal points of an investigation into school violence.

Crime scene tape borders Pearl High School in Pearl, Mississippi, after a shooting rampage by a sixteen-year-old student killed two and wounded six students. This tragedy, occurring in 1997, two years before the Columbine killings, received media attention but did little to effect swift change in gun control legislation.

Gangs in Schools

Youth gangs are consistently linked with serious crime problems in elementary and secondary schools in the United States, and since the 1970s, there has been a dramatic increase in gang activity in the country. Like the crime rate, the overall number of gangs and gang members in the United States decreased slightly in the late 1990s; the percentage of students reporting the presence of street gang members at schools decreased from 29 percent to 17 percent between 1995 and 1999. However, in medium- and large-sized cities, general gang involvement remains near peak levels, involving a total of more than 700,000 adolescents and young adults.

There is a strong relationship between the presence of gangs and guns in schools. In schools with active gangs, higher percentages of students report knowing another student who brought a gun to school and having seen a gun at school. Young people who are gang members are much more likely than other students to carry guns and to commit serious or violent crimes. Schools with gangs have almost double the rate of violent victimization at school compared to schools without a gang presence.

Gangs and guns go hand in hand. In this photograph, unidentified members of a Los Angeles gang called Diamond Street proudly pose for the camera.

Guns and Schools

Since two out of every five American households own a gun, it's not surprising to find that some students bring firearms to school. However, studies vary widely on how frequently this occurs and whether or not guns have become commonplace at some schools. In 1990, the Centers for Disease Control (CDC) found that one in twenty students carried a gun to high school in the previous thirty-day period. Seven years later, another survey reported that 6 percent of high school students carried a gun during the previous thirty days, and 7 percent of high school students had been threatened or injured with a weapon on school property within the last year. More than 2,800 students were expelled in the 1999–2000 school year for bringing guns to school; 43 percent of those expelled were in elementary school or junior high school. Students who were actually caught and then expelled are surely only a small proportion of those who actually carry weapons.

The National Education Association (NEA) estimates that 100,000 kids bring guns to school every day, but other estimates place the number closer to 20,000. Homicide or suicide on school grounds is not widespread. However, in the years from 1993 to 2003, more than 200 students died in school-related homicides or suicides that took place in communities of all sizes. The National School Safety Center, based in California, keeps an ongoing tally of school-related violent deaths. The vast majority of these incidents take place in high schools, but approximately 10 percent of the violent deaths at schools in the last decade occurred in elementary schools. About two-thirds of the victims of this school-associated violence were students, 10 percent were teachers or other staff members, and a quarter were community members who were killed on school property. Five out of every six school-based homicide or suicide victims were boys.

Shootings on public school grounds were not a new phenomenon in the 1990s, but previously, most had taken place in impoverished urban areas and received very little sustained mainstream media coverage or political attention. The first high-profile, multiple-victim school shooting occurred at Grover Cleveland Elementary School in San Diego, California, on January 29, 1979, when a sixteen-year-old girl opened fire on an elementary school playground with a high-powered rifle. When asked why, she stated, "I don't like Mondays. This livens up the day."

Despite the short-term publicity that may follow when children fire guns at their classmates in school, the fact remains that less than 1 percent of all homicides among school-aged children (five to nineteen years of age) occur in or around school grounds or on the way to and from school. In the 1980s, most Americans generally rationalized school violence as extremely isolated incidents that did not warrant concern.

Rampage School Shootings

The school shootings of the 1990s—in which middle school and high school boys killed their classmates and teachers in small cities and towns in suburban and rural areas—were different. Americans were forced to confront the fact that these murders occurred in areas where crime rates were generally low.

The majority of these school-associated killings involved a gun used by a child, and a firearm was always used in the worst of these massacres. From July 1992 to July 1999, 218 students were directly involved in a school-associated homicide or suicide. Of this number, 123 (56 percent) used at least one gun at the time of the event. Between 1992 and 2001, thirty-five incidents occurred in which students attended their school or a school-sponsored event and began firing at whoever was in attendance. These incidents scared Americans—the targets usually seemed to be chosen completely at random, with no attempt to fire the gun at selected individuals, making people feel as if this type of violence could happen anywhere and to anyone.

The first of these types of traumatic school shootings occurred in Stockton, California, on January 17, 1989, when a gunman opened fire on the crowded schoolyard at Cleveland Elementary School. The killer used an AK-47 assault rifle fitted with a magazine holding 75 bullets. After firing off 104 rounds, he killed himself, but not before he had killed five students and wounded thirty-three others. That shooting directly led to an executive order issued by President George H.W. Bush in March 1989 that prevented the importation of a number of semiautomatic firearms and sparked a push by California lawmakers that led to the state's first assault weapons ban. This incident—along with a rampage shooting in Killeen, Texas, that was not at a school—had an enormous impact on American public opinion and led directly to Congress's passage of gun control legislation such as the 1993 Brady Bill and the assault weapons ban of 1994.

Fourteen-year-olds Jedaiah Zinzo (left) and Justin Schnepp were charged as adults with conspiracy to commit murder in a plot to attack Holland Woods Middle School in Port Huron, Michigan, in 1999.

School Shootings Become Major News

A brief lull in school-associated, multiple-victim shootings followed the passage of gun control legislation, but ever more violent incidents dominated the late 1990s until it seemed that there was an epidemic of school violence. On October 1, 1997, a sixteen-year-old killed two students and wounded seven in his high school in Pearl, Mississippi. Two months later, a fourteen-year-old boy killed three students and wounded eight others in West Paducah, Kentucky. On March 24, 1998, a thirteen-year-old and an eleven-year-old killed four students and one teacher and wounded ten others in Westside Middle School in Jonesboro, Arkansas. The two middle school students set off a false fire alarm and waited in the woods next to the school to fire on their classmates and teachers as they stood outside. Two months after that, a fifteen-year-old opened fire in his high school cafeteria in Springfield, Oregon, killing two and wounding twenty-two others. The student had been arrested and released a day earlier for bringing a gun to school; that night, he murdered both his parents and then went to school the next day to kill his classmates.

OTHER INCIDENTS OF SCHOOL VIOLENCE

Moses Lake, Washington, February 2, 1996: Two students and one teacher were killed when a fourteen-year-old boy opened fire on his algebra class.

Bethel, Alaska, February 19, 1997: A sixteen-year-old killed a student and his principal and wounded two other people.

Edinboro, Pennsylvania, April 24, 1998: One teacher and two students were killed at a middle school dance by a fourteen-year-old student with a semiautomatic pistol.

Fayetteville, Tennessee, May 19, 1998: A student was killed by an eighteen-year-old honor student in the parking lot at Lincoln County High School three days before he was to graduate.

A Different Kind of Violence

In the late 1980s and early 1990s, a tremendous upsurge in youth violence occurred in many American cities. Analysts usually blamed these shootings on poverty, lack of opportunity, racial segregation, gang warfare, and turf battles in the drug trade. The new violence in suburban and rural schools seemed to be of a different type. It more closely resembled rampage shootings by adults in workplaces, post offices, restaurants, and other public spaces. A careful study of several of the school-associated murders in rural and suburban areas in the late 1990s could not link the motives of the shooters in any meaningful way. Often, the youngsters felt unhappy or angry and complained of being bullied or attacked, but the grievance was usually not very specific; instead, it was general and abstract. Ironically, rampage shootings almost never happen in inner-city schools, where gun violence usually occurs over specific concerns among individuals.

More than 90 percent of these rampage-style school shootings were committed by young white males. These boys were sometimes picked on by others and often showed warning signs of depression and suicidal tendencies; about a quarter of the students who were involved in lethal school violence committed suicide at the end of their shooting spree. Student shooters ranged in age from ten to twenty-one; the median age was sixteen. Almost all had extremely easy access to guns, and most had received training in the proper handling of firearms. On the other hand, most of the shooters were not loners; they had friends, were good students, came from intact homes, and were not considered to be at high risk for opening fire on their classmates and teachers.

The Columbine High School Massacre

By far, the most dramatic and bloody case of school violence took place at Columbine High School in Littleton, Colorado. For more than a year, an eighteen-

> **FAST FACT**
>
> The availability of guns does not cause school violence, but the replacement of knives and brass knuckles by more deadly firearms has increased the lethality of school attacks. For example, the fifteen-year-old shooter in Springfield, Oregon, sprayed the school cafeteria with fifty-one shots from a .22-caliber Ruger semiautomatic rifle, which could potentially kill many people. (Two were killed and twenty-two were wounded.) He was captured only when he stopped to reload.

Students, survivors of the Columbine High School massacre in Littleton, Colorado, share their grief following one of the deadliest school shootings in U.S. history.

year-old and a seventeen-year-old student—members of the school's so-called Trenchcoat Mafia—carefully planned their attack. In their yearbooks, videotapes, journals, and computer files, the two students listed sixty-seven students—especially athletes and minorities—whom they disliked for various reasons. They intended to kill 500 students and blow up the entire school.

On April 20, 1999, the two students, armed with sawed-off shotguns, a semiautomatic rifle, and homemade explosives, entered the school firing the shotguns and tossing pipe bombs at their fellow students. The gunmen fired their first shots at 11:19 A.M. and injured their last victim only sixteen minutes later. In the eight minutes that they were in the school library, they shot and killed ten people and wounded twelve more. By the time that their rampage had ended, the pair had killed twelve students and one teacher and wounded twenty-three others. As the police closed in on them, they committed suicide with their own guns. The murderers had placed two 20-pound (9-kilogram) propane bombs in the cafeteria; had the bombs functioned properly, all 488 people in the room might have died.

School Violence May Be Declining

The death of any child is a tragedy, but the sensational nature of the school shootings of the 1990s hid the fact that the number of crimes committed on school grounds is relatively small and declining. The total number of shootings has decreased since the 1993 school year, although the number of multiple-victim incidents seems to have increased. The number of school-associated deaths varies greatly from year to year, but the average over the last ten years has been less than forty. Over the last decade, fewer than forty of the 116,910 schools in the United States have had a multiple-victim shooting attack. A child had a greater chance of being hit by lightning (one in a million) than of being murdered on school grounds. Young people are far more likely to be killed or seriously injured when they are out of school than when they are in it.

The publicity that followed the multiple-victim school shootings of the late 1990s enraged gun advocacy groups, who felt that the violence was being used unfairly to support gun control positions. Supporters of widespread gun ownership noted that the Pearl, Mississippi, school shooter was finally apprehended by an assistant principal who held the killer at gunpoint as he was trying to flee. Likewise, the Edinboro, Pennsylvania, shooter was stopped by the owner of the banquet hall where the dance was taking place, who pointed a shotgun at him and ordered him to drop his gun. Taking note of these facts, the head of the Lethal Force Institute suggested in the *Wall Street Journal* that the best solution to school shootings was to arm schoolteachers: "[Their] weapons would have to be discreetly concealed, and which personnel are armed should be revealed only on a need-to-know basis."

School massacres with guns are not confined to the United States, but also take place in nations with much stricter gun-control laws. On March 13, 1996, forty-three-year-old Thomas Hamilton killed sixteen children and one teacher at Dunblane Primary School in Scotland. On April 28, 1999, a fourteen-year-old boy killed a student in Taber, Alberta; it was the first fatal high school shooting in Canada in twenty years. On April 26, 2002, nineteen-year-old Robert Steinhauser killed thirteen teachers, two students, and one policeman at the Johann Gutenberg secondary school in Erfurt, Germany, before killing himself.

Gun-Free School Zones

The dramatic killings in the Stockton, California, elementary school playground in 1989 led the federal government to try to prevent future gun-related incidents in America's schools. In 1990, Congress passed the Gun-Free School Zones Act. This law made it a federal crime, subject to up to five years' imprisonment and a $5,000 fine, "for any individual knowingly to possess a firearm at a place that the individual knows, or has reasonable cause to believe, is a school zone." Congress defined a school zone as "in, or on the grounds of, a public, parochial or private school; or within a distance of 1,000 feet [300 meters] from the grounds of a

public, parochial or private school." Federal, state, and local authorities were encouraged to post signs around school zones warning that the possession of firearms was prohibited in the area.

Under the U.S. Constitution, the United States is set up as a federal system. This means that power is divided between the state and national governments. Schools and education are usually controlled by the state governments and not the national government. Congress, however, relied on the authority of the commerce clause of the Constitution (which deals with control of interstate trade) to justify the passage of the Gun-Free School Zones Act. The lawmakers knew that tighter control of guns would not eliminate violence, but they hoped that it would make it more difficult to commit crimes and shoot people on and around school grounds.

School violence continues even after the shocking tragedy at Columbine High School in Colorado. This photograph shows a memorial set up by mourners after a school shooting at Santana High School in Santee, California, in 2001.

United States v. Lopez

In 1992, Alfonso Lopez Jr. was a twelfth-grade student at Edison High School in San Antonio, Texas. On an anonymous tip, school authorities searched Lopez and discovered that he was carrying a .38-caliber handgun and five bullets. He was sentenced to six months in prison; his appeal eventually reached the U.S. Supreme Court. Lopez argued that the federal government had no authority to make laws regarding control of the public schools. He was

Chief Justice William Rehnquist listening to arguments in the Alfonso Lopez Jr. case.

supported by the National Rifle Association (NRA) and several other groups who claimed that Congress was not using the commerce power of the Constitution properly when it passed the Gun-Free School Zones Act. Opponents of the act believed in the goal of reducing school violence but insisted that Congress could not regulate guns in schools because it could not reasonably link firearms possession and interstate commerce.

On April 26, 1995, a sharply divided Supreme Court voted five to four to declare the law unconstitutional as an improper exercise of power by Congress. Chief Justice William Rehnquist, writing for the Court, stated that "the possession of a gun in a local school zone is in no sense an economic activity" that might have an effect on interstate commerce. The majority of the justices believed that if Congress could regulate all activities that might lead to violent crime, it would "convert congressional authority under the commerce clause to a general police power of the sort retained by the States." The dissenters in *Lopez* noted the close connection between gun violence in schools and the movement of guns in interstate commerce as part of the illegal drug trade. Justice Stephen Breyer argued that Congress's regulation of guns in the schools was no different than its power to keep them free of controlled substances, asbestos, and alcohol.

The decision in *Lopez* was one of the few times since the 1930s that the Supreme Court has declared a national law unconstitutional on the grounds that it violated state rights. However, the principle became one of the hallmarks of the Supreme Court under Chief Justice Rehnquist. Some feeble attempts have been made by Congress to pass modified national gun-free schools legislation by adding the requirement that the government must prove that a firearm has "moved in or the possession of such firearm otherwise affects interstate or foreign commerce." These attempts have not been successful, and the right to pass such laws has fallen to individual states.

FAST FACT

Teenagers were not particularly supportive of the suggestion to arm teachers and principals. In a recent survey, more than 90 percent responded "no" to the statement "Teachers and principals should be able to bring handguns to school to protect students."

As of 2003, more than forty states had passed legislation outlawing possession of firearms on or near—usually within 1,000 feet (300 meters) of—school grounds (with some exceptions, such as for the possession of firearms in one's own home).

These state laws do not meet with universal favor. Some gun advocacy groups favor the arming of selected school employees as the best way to stop future school shootings. One law school professor stated that "by and large, American schools are 'gun free.' That's why criminals are free to murder students there without fear of facing opposition." The executive director of Gun Owners of America (GOA), a gun advocacy group, discussing a school shooting in New Orleans, Louisiana, in 2003, stated, "This tragedy might have been prevented by the presence of armed teachers and other employees at the school."

The Limited Impact of Columbine

The Columbine High School massacre of 1999 led to a great deal of soul-searching in Washington, D.C. Politicians blamed the seeming increase in school violence on everything from reactions to overmedication to the entertainment industry's glorification of violence to long-term ill effects of day care. The wave of school shootings raised anxiety levels in most communities in the United States. School boards closely examined school safety and, in many cases, greatly increased the level of security in order to avoid another Littleton.

A variety of techniques were tried to prevent guns from being smuggled into schools: metal detectors, armed security guards, razor-wire fences, and frequent searches of lockers and students' personal belongings. Schools also paid greater attention to and acted on students' threatening language, unique clothing and hairstyles, and perceived antisocial behavior. Many schools were quick to use Columbine as an excuse to enforce conformity in the classroom. One student in Virginia was suspended for dying his hair blue; the school official justified the suspension by claiming, "The school administration has ruled that students who wear unusual or unique hair colors, such as blue or green, are to be removed from school.... In view of the circumstances that have occurred recently, the governor expressed that unusual activities/appearances should not be ignored."

Nonetheless, school shooting incidents did not cease. Only a month after the massacre at Columbine, a student opened fire on his classmates in a crowded hallway at

One of the many shootings in the wake of Columbine occurred in Red Lion, Pennsylvania, where a fourteen-year-old shot and killed his principal and then turned the gun on himself. Mourners leave the Red Lion Bible Church after the funeral of gunman James Sheets.

Heritage High School in Conyers, Georgia, wounding six students. On November 19, 1999, a twelve-year-old shot and killed a student at Deming Middle School in Deming, New Mexico. A month later, four students were wounded when a thirteen-year-old opened fire with a semiautomatic handgun at Fort Gibson Middle School in Oklahoma. In May 2000, on the last day of classes at Lake Worth Middle School in Florida, a thirteen-year-old shot and killed a teacher with a semiautomatic pistol. In March 2001, a fifteen-year-old firing from a bathroom at Santana High School in Santee, California, killed two and wounded thirteen. In April 2003, a fourteen-year-old killed his school principal inside the crowded cafeteria of Red Lion Area Junior High School in York, Pennsylvania, and then killed himself with a second handgun. In 2000, just days before the one-year anniversary of the Columbine shooting, a poll revealed that 70 percent of Americans believed such a shooting could occur at a school in their own community.

In 1999, President Bill Clinton's administration, joined by many in Congress, supported renewed gun control measures. The push seemed to have popular support, symbolized by a "Million Mom March" on Mother's Day, May 14, 2000. Hundreds of thousands of mothers (and others) gathered in Washington, D.C., and elsewhere to call on lawmakers to pass stricter gun control laws. Yet despite the outrage after the Columbine massacre, no new measures were passed by Congress. The terrorist attacks on the United States in September 2001, followed by the American invasions of Afghanistan and Iraq, pushed the issue of school violence into the background.

Metal Detectors in Schools

Some school officials have turned to the use of metal detectors to try to keep guns out of school buildings. According to a 1994 survey by the National School Boards Association, metal detectors were being used in about 15 percent of all school districts, and the number has probably increased in the last ten years. However, the use of metal detectors as a way to search for firearms can be controversial. Metal detector searches of students have led to legal challenges under the Fourth Amendment to the Constitution, which guarantees that individuals should be free from unreasonable searches and seizures.

In the historic case of *Tinker v. Des Moines,* the U.S. Supreme Court ruled in 1969 that students do not "shed their constitutional rights...at the schoolhouse gate." Justice Abe Fortas wrote in his decision, "In our system, state-operated schools may not be enclaves of totalitarianism. School officials do not possess absolute authority over their students. Students in school as well as out of school are 'persons' under our Constitution." In 1985, the landmark *T.L.O.* case (the name is based on the initials of the minor involved) held that school officials and administrators must have "a reasonable suspicion"

Metal detectors can be an effective way to keep firearms out of schools, but their legality and use are often challenged under the Fourth Amendment.

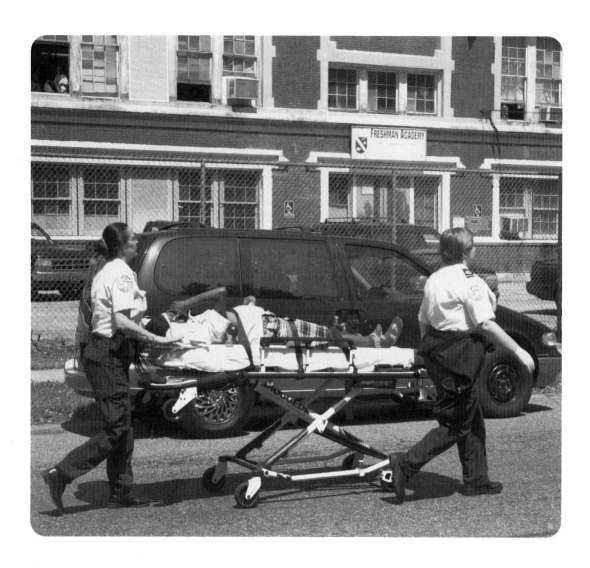

Easy availability of guns makes U.S. schools vulnerable to those wishing to cause harm inside and outside of school grounds. In 2003, an unidentified gunman entered the neighborhood surrounding John McDonogh High School in New Orleans, Louisiana, and shot one student and wounded three others.

that a student is carrying a gun or intends to break the law before that student may be searched. However, the Supreme Court specifically refused to explain what constituted a legal student search by school officials.

Court cases involving metal detector searches for guns in the schools are rare. In *People v. Dukes*, Tawana Dukes, a student at Washington Irving High School in New York City, was charged with criminal possession of a weapon. She attempted to suppress the evidence from a metal detector search on the grounds that it violated her Fourth Amendment rights. A criminal court in New York City disagreed. The court emphasized that the intrusion was very small compared to the school's important interest in preventing acts and threats of violence. The court stated, "Weapons in schools, like terrorist bombings at airports and courthouses, are dangers which demand an appropriate response."

Rather than using the test for reasonableness as outlined in the *T.L.O.* decision, the *Dukes* court instead claimed that this metal detector search was a type of administrative search intended to prevent a dangerous occurrence. Therefore, it was aimed at a group or class of people (in this case, students) and did not require individualized suspicion. The *Dukes* court compared this type of "administrative" search to those using scanning devices in public buildings such as airports and courthouses, or highway checkpoints for drunken drivers. Those types of searches were allowed by the Supreme Court in a six to three vote in *Michigan Department of State Police v. Sitz* in 1990.

Most court decisions that dealt with metal detector searches since *Dukes* (for example, those in Illinois, Pennsylvania, and Arkansas) have agreed with the New York court. In 1996, a Florida court even expanded this concept of administrative searches. In this case, a high school with an open campus began a policy allowing random searches of students in classrooms with handheld metal detector wands. An independent security team hired by the school district entered one room to perform a search and observed students passing a jacket to the back of the room. The officers confiscated the jacket and found a gun. A Florida court of appeals ruled that the compelling need for security in schools permitted this type of search, which did not require probable cause.

> **FAST FACT**
>
> In upholding the constitutionality of the metal detector search, the court in *Dukes* said that New York had clearly demonstrated a need for conducting such searches: "According to school records, over 2,000 weapons were recovered [from city schools] in the 1990–91 school year alone.... If schools cannot operate in a violence-free atmosphere, the education will suffer, a result which ultimately threatens the well-being of everyone."

Random Student Gun Searches

According to recent court decisions, metal detector searches for guns seem to be constitutional if security guards follow "a very detailed script" based upon guidelines adopted by the head of the public school system. For example, students should be searched by officers of the same sex; also, officers must search all students, unless lines become too long, and even then, there must be an identifiable pattern to a random search. An officer is not permitted to select any one particular student unless there is reasonable suspicion that the student has a weapon.

However, not all searches are conducted this way. Since 1994, officials at Los Angeles public middle schools and high schools have carried out random searches of students on a daily basis. The policy followed two separate shooting incidents in which students died when classmates pulled out guns in class and shot them. The school district claims that the program has been very successful as a deterrent. However, at Locke High School in South Central Los Angeles, students formed the Locke Student Union to challenge the Los Angeles policy. They claimed that students were frequently searched against their will, without warning, and in front of other students. Students felt humiliated when subjected to searches and began resenting school officials; the school felt more like a jail, students felt, than an institution of learning. Nonetheless, the Los Angeles policy still remained in place in 2004.

> **FAST FACT**
>
> Statistics can often be used to support either side of a debate. Only 43 guns were found in Los Angeles schools in 1999–2000, compared to 151 in 1993–1994. On the other hand, nearly ten years of random searching has failed to turn up a single gun. (The guns that have been recovered were found in ways other than random searches.)

Safe Storage at Home

From July 1, 1992, to June 30, 1999, a total of 358 school-associated violent deaths occurred in the United States. After a careful study, the CDC concluded that the majority of the guns used in these events were obtained from the shooters' homes or from friends or relatives. Students who committed a school-associated suicide or a multiple-victim homicide were more likely to have obtained firearms from their homes than from any other source. Although mental-health issues are obviously a cause in school shootings, the ease of obtaining a gun paves a road to serious violence. At-risk students may exhibit aggressive, defiant, or other oppositional behavior, but they can rarely kill more than one person in a school without the aid of a firearm.

Because guns are present in about two out of every five American households, gaining access to a gun is rarely difficult for a good proportion of young people. Although many states restrict gun ownership by young people, this usually does not pose any difficulty. Interviews after the school shooting in Conyers, Georgia, indicated that most households in the neighborhood owned some sort of

Making the public aware of how danger from firearms has infiltrated even the most affluent neighborhoods is one goal of gun safety groups. This sign hung along a wall on the Massachusetts Turnpike in Boston in 2003 reminds people never to take gun safety for granted.

FAST FACT

The worst incident of mass murder of children in the United States took place on May 18, 1927. On that day, forty-five people, mostly children, were killed and fifty-eight were injured when a disgruntled school board member, Andrew Kehoe, dynamited the new school building in Bath, Michigan. He wanted revenge for the foreclosure of his farm, which was caused in part by the taxes he was required to pay for the new school.

firearm, and gun usage was an accepted way of life for young people of the area. Most Conyers students claimed that they could easily acquire a gun within fifteen minutes to an hour, and many had witnessed disputes between individuals at which a gun was displayed and waved around.

A committee examining youth violence in schools concluded that in every one of the school shootings investigated, the attacks

> were committed by youth armed with rifles and handguns who were breaking current gun laws.... Both state and federal laws prohibit children of this age from possessing or carrying guns without adult supervision.... Even the most fervent champions of the rights of citizens to own guns have stood for keeping them away from unsupervised children. Nevertheless, research has shown that more than half of privately owned firearms are insecurely stored. Insecure storage of firearms was clearly a factor in four of these six cases.

Grunow v. Valor Corporation of Florida

In November 2002, a jury awarded an astonishing $24 million verdict in a case brought by the family of Florida middle school teacher Barry Grunow, who was killed in his classroom by a thirteen-year-old student with a seventy-five-dollar handgun. The complaint, filed for $75 million in October 2000, attempted to assign the responsibility to several parties, including Valor Corporation, a wholesale gun distributor and dealer. The plaintiff argued that Valor had sold the gun that was used in the fatal shooting and that the gun was unreasonably dangerous and defective because it lacked a locking system to prevent unauthorized use by minors.

The jury verdict put 45 percent of the blame on the local school board for allowing the shooter to return to school after being suspended and 50 percent on the elderly friend who owned the gun and kept it in a cookie tin in a drawer. However, the jury also found Valor 5 percent negligent and ordered the gun distributor to pay $1.2 million. The verdict was the first against a gun seller for distributing inexpensive guns without "feasible safety features" to prevent their use by children and other unauthorized people. The jury verdict was invalidated by the judge, however, and the case is currently under appeal.

The Committee to Study Youth Violence

Following the shootings at Columbine High School, Congress requested that the National Research Council study the question of lethal violence in American schools. The Committee to Study Youth Violence was established in 2001 to examine specific case studies, study the causes

A picture of Barry Grunow and his family is displayed during the trial in the case of Grunow v. Valor Corporation of Florida. Grunow's widow, Pamela Grunow, successfully sued the gun manufacturer for selling a weapon that is unreasonably dangerous because it has no safety device. Barry Grunow was killed in 2000 by one of his students using this type of gun.

and consequences of these shootings, and suggest actions by individuals or institutions to prevent such events from occurring in the future.

In its 2003 report, the committee admitted that it was "virtually impossible to identify the likely offenders in advance" or even to develop an accurate profile of students at high risk to commit these kinds of shootings. The committee therefore concluded that "these young people had such easy access to firearms...[that] it is necessary to find more effective means than we have of realizing the nation's long established policy goal of keeping firearms out of the hands of unsupervised children and out of our schools." Nonetheless, because guns are so much a part of American culture, whether in the countryside, the suburbs, or the cities, actual policy proposals to limit the ability of young people to acquire firearms not only have yet to meet with widespread acceptance but are vehemently opposed by some people.

CHAPTER 4

Protecting Children?

Because children—especially boys—seem to be drawn to guns, all parents and adults need to take common-sense steps to protect children. In households that do not own firearms, talking to children about guns is sufficient; young people simply need to be reminded constantly that guns can cause real injuries and that no one is invincible. Younger children must be taught never to touch a gun and always to tell an adult if they come across one. In households that do own firearms, common sense means unloading and locking all guns so that a child or teen cannot gain access to them without direct adult supervision.

Many adults support greater government regulation of firearms. To a certain degree, an emphasis on the safety of children represents a brilliant tactical decision by gun control advocates. Many Americans distrust the term *gun control* because it represents a loss of freedom of choice and implies that some citizens are not careful, mature, or stable enough to own handguns. An accent on *safety* instead of *control* is a much less controversial and popular position; after all, who's against the safety of children? Gun control appeals that involve the death of children are far more effective than statistical discussions of crime and self-defense. For example, the Bell Campaign was a national organization of parents, some of whose children were killed by guns, that advocated stricter gun laws. Their demonstrations usually included ringing of bells for every child killed by a gun that year.

By shifting the debate to "protecting children," who, of course, do not speak for themselves, gun control supporters attempted to counter their image as supporters of big government, and possibly even of dictatorship. On the other hand, it's indisputable that there is a public health and safety issue surrounding children and guns. In 2000, approximately 1,500 Americans under the age of eighteen died as a result of firearms, including 819 murders, 537 suicides, and 150 accidents, and many of the murderers were themselves teenagers with guns.

Unsafe Firearms Storage

About 40 percent of American households have made the very serious decision to keep a gun in the home. Most Americans who own guns use them for hunting, shooting sports, home security, or personal defense. National research shows that more than one-third of the homes with children younger than eighteen (representing 22 million children in 11 million homes) reported having at least one gun (usually a handgun) in the house.

For children, the risks of unsafe firearms storage practices can sometimes be a matter of life and death for themselves and for others. Numerous tragedies occur involving unlocked firearms that are easily accessible to young people, either at their own homes or the homes of relatives or neighbors. These incidents might very well never happen if the adults in these children's lives unloaded and locked their firearms and ammunition so

Various locking devices for firearms are both easy and inexpensive to purchase.

Gun owners are a large and vocal group, many of whom believe that gun control laws violate their constitutional rights. In Boston in 1999, a rally calling for the repeal of a landmark Massachusetts gun control law drew a supporting crowd of thousands.

that the children could not take and use them so easily. In most accidents and suicides, and in many homicides, the firearms that were used were found at home.

Many children live in homes with guns that are stored when loaded and placed within easy access. Among households with children and firearms, almost half had at least one unlocked firearm (meaning that the gun was not in a locked place or not locked with a trigger lock or other locking mechanism). Overall, about 10 percent of adults with children kept firearms unlocked and loaded, and 4 percent kept them unlocked, unloaded, and stored with ammunition. Therefore, adults in almost 15 percent of American homes with children and firearms—about 1.5 million homes with 2.5 million children—stored firearms in such a way that any child who wanted to could get a loaded gun.

These figures probably underrepresent the number of guns stored in such a manner, although it's difficult to even estimate the number of gun-owning households with children or how their guns are stored. One study noted that in gun-owning households with children, completely different answers about gun storage were received depending upon who answered the questions. In the same household, three times as many gun owners (usually married men) as nongun owners (usually their wives) reported that a gun was stored loaded, while four times as many reported that a household gun was stored loaded and unlocked. Because nongun owners were much more likely to be female, it appears that many women may be unaware that guns in their homes are stored loaded or loaded and unlocked in a manner that most experts agree is unsafe.

To ensure the safety of children, most people agree that guns in a home should always be locked up and stored unloaded so that a child or teen cannot use them without direct adult supervision. In addition, the ammunition should be locked and stored separately, and keys should be hidden where kids are unable to find them. Handguns in particular need to be stored carefully, because they are much more likely to be kept where children can get to them. According to several studies, about half of all handguns are stored in bedrooms, where it is easy for children to find them.

The majority of both gun-owning and nongun-owning parents support safe storage as the best way to prevent children from being injured by firearms. Some gun owners, however, insist that "loaded guns can be good for kids." They argue that fatal gun accidents in the United States involving children are relatively rare; this seems to demonstrate that most Americans already treat guns with respect and educate their children about firearms safety. In the year 2000, there were approximately twenty fatal gun accidents involving children aged under one year to four, twenty more for those aged five to nine, and less than fifty more for kids aged ten to fourteen. These fatalities must be weighed against the positive benefits of having a gun available for self-defense. Of

> **FAST FACT**
>
> At the other end of the gun storage spectrum, almost 40 percent of American families kept firearms locked, unloaded, and separate from ammunition. The people most likely to store firearms in this manner were those with a child five to nine years old, having at least a four-year college education, or having an income of more than $65,000 per year.

course, some gun owners contend that parents must teach gun safety to children, but after that, most responsible older children can be trusted with a loaded gun. In one recent study, a quarter of parents of four- to twelve-year-olds believed that their children could, in fact, be trusted with a loaded gun.

Gun Safes

There are several different ways to safely store or lock firearms in order to prevent children and other unauthorized people from using them. These mechanisms usually depend on keys, keypads, or combination locks to limit access to firearms. In the early 1900s, guns were displayed for everyone to see in beautiful wood racks or cabinets with fine etched glass. The rise in violence in the late twentieth century may be one factor that put an end to most of these types of displays. Today, many owners lock up their guns to keep them out of the hands of criminals, the untrained, the curious, and the impulsive.

Most people use the same hiding places for guns, and some studies indicate that burglars (and by extension, children) can find a gun to steal within four minutes of entering a house or apartment. Because there's almost no place to "hide" a gun where it could not be found, fixed location storage containers, such as gun lockers, cases, cabinets, and safes, generally provide the greatest security against misuse. Of course, a gun safe is only as secure as the location of the keys or combination; parents often mistakenly believe that their children don't know where the keys to unlock gun safes are kept.

One recent advertisement for a gun safe attempted to state its advantages in a way that would entice gun owners.

Quick access gun boxes for fast, simple, access for authorized users, and excellent protection against unauthorized use by children or adults. Choose from a variety of permanent or portable versions, (some are both!), sized for hand guns, rifles, or

shotguns. Your last excuse for not owning a proper
gun safe or locker is gone! Remember, the typical
gun safe is sold after a burglary, fire, or an accident.

*Project HomeSafe, a
nationwide firearms
safety education program,
distributed over 20,000
free safety locks in 2002
to publicize its efforts.*

Gun Locks

Though gun safes provide the greatest security, many
people prefer locks. Many adults own guns for defensive
purposes and believe that if they stored their guns in safes,
they would not be able to use them fast enough in case of
emergency. At the same time, they know that an easily
available gun is a tempting target for children. A *trigger lock*
is a type of safety lock that can prevent a gun's trigger
from firing either by accident or by an unauthorized user.
There are a variety of internal locks on guns that can do
this. One type is normally mounted in the grip of the gun
and either locks the manual thumb safety into place or

prevents the hammer from moving. Another type, the internal trigger block, uses a blocking pin to prevent the firing mechanism from moving inside the gun.

In addition, several types of locks can be added to guns after they are purchased. An external trigger block, a piece of metal that fits between the rear of the trigger and the trigger guard, prevents the gun from firing. Some people simply use a standard key or combination lock placed behind the trigger in order to accomplish the same result. Gun owners can also use a type of external trigger lock that completely covers the trigger mechanism on either side with two metal or plastic pieces that clamp around the trigger guard. Another type of safety lock is a barrel-and-chamber insert, which uses metal or plastic cables, plugs, pins, or rods that fit down the barrel of the gun and block the chamber.

A local resident of Cedar Rapids, Iowa, examines a cable-style safety lock.

In all cases, the goal of safety locks is the same: to prevent people, especially children, from using guns when they don't have permission to do so. Gun safety advocates believe that trigger locks are an inexpensive way to prevent guns kept in the home from being operated by unsupervised children. They believe that the locks reduce the number of unintentional firearms deaths and suicides occurring each year and perhaps even cut down on the number of youth homicides. Polls generally show that three out of four Americans, including gun owners, support a mandatory requirement that gun manufacturers include child safety locks on all new handguns.

No federal law requires that guns have locking devices. Because Congress exempted guns from regulation by the Consumer Products Safety Commission, there are not even any national safety standards for safety locks. However, several states require that some form of locking device be included with every firearm sold by a licensed gun dealer. California's law, which went into effect in January 2002, required that all handguns sold in California must include an approved firearm safety device, such as a trigger lock or safety box, for safe storage. The law began the first testing standards for locking devices; only devices officially approved by California satisfy that state's requirement for locking devices to be included with every gun sold in the state. Despite fears by California gun dealers that the firearms safety law would hurt business, sales of handguns in California were not affected in any way, even increasing slightly from 2001 to 2003. Massachusetts and Washington, D.C., both require that almost all firearms be secured with locking devices; Maryland, Michigan, and New Jersey all require locking devices on handguns only.

Child Safety and Self-Defense

Some gun owners don't use trigger locks for reasons of self-defense. A gun owner can unlock a gun within

FAST FACT

In 1997, voters in the state of Washington overwhelmingly rejected Initiative 676, a gun control measure backed by billionaire software developer Bill Gates that would have required state handgun owners to take safety tests and buy trigger locks in order to purchase a handgun. The vote was 69 percent opposed and 31 percent in favor of the initiative.

seconds only if the key is stored near the gun. However, this would mean that children could also unlock the gun in seconds if they discovered the combination or the location of the key. An adult could prevent a child from finding a key by hiding it elsewhere, but then the gun could not easily be unlocked in seconds. Gun Owners of America (GOA) strongly opposed gun safety locks in principle. The organization pointed to occasions when crime victims could not defend themselves because they could not get access to guns that they knew how to use. In one case, a fourteen-year-old babysitter in Merced, California, who had training in firearms, had to flee the house rather than shoot an intruder, because she couldn't get to locked-up guns. The attacker, armed only with a pitchfork and without any known motive, then killed two of the children in the house. After the murders, the babysitter's uncle blasted California legislators for passing safe storage laws that forced the parents to place the gun in a way that was not accessible to children: "If only [Jessica] had a gun available to her, she could have stopped the whole thing. If she had been properly armed, she could have stopped [the attacker] in his tracks."

Representatives of the firearms industry also believe that locks will increase the price of guns and probably won't make a difference. "A kid, if he wants to, will figure out how it works," stated one opponent of mandatory trigger locks. A trigger lock program in Edinboro, Pennsylvania, the site of a particularly bloody school shooting in 1998, was rejected by most residents. Even though the murderer had had easy accessibility to his father's semiautomatic handgun, residents continued to believe after the massacre that trigger locks were useless for a gun kept at home for self-defense. Instead, they insisted that it was a family responsibility to teach respect for firearms.

The Ups and Downs of Project HomeSafe

Many organizations in the United States provide inexpensive trigger lock distribution programs, often through local police departments. For example, the SAFE KIDS program works through grassroots organizations to furnish low-cost locks for the prevention of unintentional firearm injury to children under age fifteen. Programs of this nature may have contributed to the dramatic reduction of the unintentional death rate for children under age fourteen by 40 percent from 1987 to 2000.

The best-known of the safety lock distribution programs is Project HomeSafe, a nationwide program

Cedar Rapids, Iowa, resident Larry Edwards picks up safety locks during Project HomeSafe's tour of the state.

FAST FACT

Safety locks fit most, but not all, guns. A child safety lock can be purchased in virtually any gun store for less than twenty-five dollars, but they are often available from gun safety organizations for free or at a lower cost.

developed by the National Shooting Sports Foundation (NSSF). The NSSF, a gun owner's organization, promotes safe firearms handling and storage practices by sponsoring safety education messages and providing free gun locking devices. Project HomeSafe was originally funded by the NSSF and then received a grant from the U.S. Department of Justice. In 2002, Project HomeSafe purchased more than 2 million firearms safety devices and distributed every one across forty-four states. The program raised gun owners' awareness of firearms safety and responsibility while avoiding legislative efforts to force gun manufacturers to equip all new firearms with gun locks.

In 2003, the Department of Justice announced that the NSSF would run Project ChildSafe, a nationwide firearms safety program backed by a $50 million grant from the federal government. Project ChildSafe works with governors and local law enforcement to provide millions of free firearms safety kits with gun locking devices to families across the United States. President George W. Bush supported a similar program when he was governor of Texas and pledged to expand its scope and support if he was elected president. The goal is to reduce gun violence by encouraging safe handling and proper storage of firearms in the home.

For example, in May 2003, Project ChildSafe donated 33,000 safety locks to the members of the New York City Police Department—enough for every member of the department. The head of the New York Police Officer's Union stated,

> A gun is simply a tool of the trade in the policing profession that carries with it a tremendous responsibility. A recent tragedy involving a police officer's child reminds us that we must take every possible precaution when our weapons are at home. This simple locking device is very effective in protecting our families, particularly children, against the possibility of discharge.

Because there are no federal standards on trigger locks, their quality varies widely. Some guns with trigger locks can still fire if loaded. Other types of trigger locks can be easily broken or otherwise overcome. In 2001, the Consumer Product Safety Commission (CPSC) tested thirty-two locks and found that children could open all but two of them without a key; in some cases, the kids simply used a paper clip. The same year, the CPSC pressured the NSSF to voluntarily recall the 400,000 free locks that it had given to gun owners as part of its Project HomeSafe campaign for safe gun storage. The CPSC claimed, and NSSF eventually agreed, that the locks were defective.

In 2000, Virginians Against Handgun Violence held a press conference to express concerns regarding gun control legislation. Dr. Peg Dolan holds up a teddy bear to explain that there are more safety regulations governing the manufacture of the bear than of guns.

The Child Safety Lock Act

Because many gun owners resist using trigger locks either out of personal principle, philosophical opposition, or just plain laziness, some politicians have tried to force their hand. A child safety lock bill, sponsored by Herb Kohl, a Democratic senator from Wisconsin, would require that all new handguns be sold with separate child safety devices or trigger locks. The proposed law also includes standards for safety locks. The Senate approved this bill in 1999 by a bipartisan vote of seventy-eight to twenty, but the measure stalled in a House-Senate Conference on juvenile crime legislation.

In support of the bill, Kohl cited a survey of 400 Wisconsin police chiefs and sheriffs in 2000, almost 90 percent of whom responded that child safety locks should be sold with each gun. Noting "the consistently high

Senator Herb Kohl, a Democrat from Wisconsin, aggressively promotes gun control legislation.

public support for this measure," Kohl stated that "this is not all that we can do, nor is it everything that needs to be done on the issue of gun safety. Nonetheless, mandatory child safety locks will save lives, especially the lives of children." Attorney General John Ashcroft expressed the Bush administration's support for the measure, stating that if Congress were to pass legislation regarding mandatory child safety locks, the president would sign it. GOA, which supports fewer restrictions on gun ownership, listed the Kohl bill as an "anti-gun" bill that needed to be defeated. As of early 2004, the legislation still had not been passed.

Children and Firearms Education

The National Rifle Association (NRA), the most powerful gun owners' advocacy group, states clearly that it "is not opposed to trigger locks; however, we do believe they can provide a false sense of security." Instead, educational programs "provide the best assurance that a firearm accident will be avoided." Many gun owners claim that the best way to keep children from gaining access to guns is simple: keep the firearms locked and unloaded in a place that children can't get to, and store the ammunition in a separate place, also out of kids' reach. This common-sense advice, combined with gun safety classes, is all that is needed to keep firearms deaths to a minimum. According to these gun owners, the government should not involve itself in firearms regulation unless a crime is committed, but instead, leave these decisions to parents.

Many organizations offer gun safety lessons. Local police departments often provide gun safety classes for students or sponsor in-school seminars. Gun owners must take the responsibility of knowing how to safely secure their weapons, because gun sellers generally offer potential buyers little or no education about safe storage of handguns. In a 2002 study in the *Archives of Pediatrics and Adolescent Medicine,* researchers made ninety-six visits to gun dealers. When asked what a consumer should know about purchasing a handgun, 85 percent of salespeople did not mention safe storage. Less than 10 percent offered advice that included all of the following: keeping the gun securely locked, keeping it unloaded, and storing it separately from the ammunition. More than 90 percent did not have any handgun safe storage educational materials on site. The widely shared assumption, which is probably incorrect, is that purchasers of handguns are already knowledgeable about the necessity of safe storage.

Eddie Eagle

Eddie Eagle, a program run by the NRA, is one of the most widely used gun safety programs for children in America. The Eddie Eagle Program was developed in 1989; by 2003, it had reached more than 20 million children in all fifty states, Canada, and Puerto Rico. The program uses a cartoon character named Eddie Eagle to teach elementary

---

TALKING ABOUT GUNS

With guns in about two out of every five American households, it's extremely likely that any child knows someone whose parents own a gun. Whether or not there's a gun in the household, it is crucial that parents talk to their children about gun safety as early as possible. There is no certain or even recommended age when a parent should bring up this topic with a child. One expert suggests that the best time to discuss guns is once a child begins to either engage in gun play or talk about guns seen at a friend's house, on television, or in the movies. When parents decide that a child is old enough to learn preliminary gun safety, they should let the child hold a gun and teach the fundamental rules of gun safety:

- Avoid guns without adult supervision.

- Never touch a gun at a friend's house or in an unfamiliar setting.

- Point a gun in a safe direction; never point it at yourself or at other people.

- Keep your finger away from the trigger.

- Never assume that the safety is on or that the gun is safe because the safety is on.

- Never assume that the gun is unloaded, even if someone else assures you that it is unloaded.

school children four important steps to take if they find or even see a gun.

The NRA states that "Eddie Eagle neither offers nor asks for any value judgment concerning firearms. Like swimming pools, electrical outlets, matchbooks and household poison, they're treated simply as a fact of life. With firearms found in about half of all American households, it's a stance that makes sense." The NRA claims that Eddie Eagle is never shown touching a firearm, nor does he appear where firearms are being used or sold. He does not promote firearms ownership or use. The Eddie Eagle Program is offered for a small fee and is used by schools, law enforcement agencies, and other groups concerned with the safety of children.

The NRA gun safety mascot, Eddie Eagle, stands beside an NRA executive at a news conference. The mascot program has come under fire from gun safety advocates who believe that the NRA is using a child-friendly image to make danger from firearms seem innocuous.

Of course, not everyone sees a program offered by the NRA as being neutral on guns. The Violence Policy Center (VPC), a gun control organization, believes that the main goal of the Eddie Eagle Program is really to protect the interests of the firearms industry by making

STOP!

Don't touch.
Leave the area.
Tell an adult.

guns more acceptable to children and youth. The VPC claims that the program employs appealing cartoon characters to put a friendly face on a hazardous product and uses Eddie Eagle as a tool to prevent the passage of child access prevention (CAP) and mandatory trigger lock laws. The VPC says that the Eddie Eagle Program places the responsibility for gun safety on children themselves, rather than recognizing that adults often store firearms irresponsibly, putting children at risk.

Guns at the Neighbor's Place

When a child goes to a friend's home to play, parents might ask the host to limit the snacks or the television. Very few parents, however, ask if there is a gun in the house and whether it is locked up. About two out of every five American households with children have guns in the house, and many of those guns—perhaps as many as half—are kept either unlocked or loaded. That means that many children play in a place with an easily accessible gun.

Parents often feel awkward about this issue. Should they keep silent and hope that their children won't find a gun or play with it, or should they speak to the other parents? One parent, who called a neighbor to ask about the storage of his gun before his children visited, stated,

I have no idea how he felt about the conversation, but I felt like an idiot. How embarrassing—confronting a stranger about his gun. Asking him about something that he has the right to own and use. But I wasn't an idiot. I did the right thing. From that day on, I knew there was a gun in that house, and I knew that it was locked up tight.

In 2000, a group of organizations headed by the American Academy of Pediatrics (AAP) began the Asking Saves Kids (ASK) Campaign. This campaign suggested that before sending a child over to play at a neighbor's, parents should ask if the neighbor has a gun in the home, and if so, how it is stored. Parents can ask this along with other questions normally discussed, such as sickness or allergies, before sending children to someone's house. Although a problem is unlikely, there are countless tragic

Stephen Sliwa, president of Colt Manufacturing Company, displays a prototype of the company's "smart gun." The technology allowing the manufacture of a gun that can be used only by the person who purchased it is still at least two years away.

stories of kids finding guns that parents thought were well hidden. The ASK Campaign recommends that parents be factual and not emotional; if there is a gun stored in an unsafe manner, or the other parent will not respond, parents can invite the other child to play at their own house. If someone gets angry when asked about gun storage, ASK hints that the person's home is not a place that parents would want their children to enter in the first place.

This photograph illustrates the curiosity most young children would feel upon discovering a hidden handgun.

"The message of the ASK Campaign is an important one to include when talking to parents about safety," said AAP president Stephen Edwards, because "many pediatricians have seen firsthand the tragic outcomes of firearm injuries to children." However, some gun owners believe that the ASK campaign is actually more about restricting guns than protecting children. One gun owner stated, "I smell the gun-control people, and their intentions are not to help children but to control all guns within the country, under the guise of helping children."

Unsafe Guns and Kids

Guns are exempt from federal American health and safety requirements, unlike virtually all other products used by children, from teddy bears to car seats. The Consumer Product Safety Commission, established in 1972 by the Consumer Product Safety Act, regulates most consumer products. The law's definition of the term *consumer product,* however, specifically excluded firearms and ammunition. As a result, the federal government has no authority to require the placement of safety features on firearms, although firearms imported from other countries must meet minimum safety standards. No federal agency can recall guns that contain safety-related defects that might affect children or adults.

Most firearms work exactly as they are designed to work, but some contain defects in design or manufacture that make it possible for them to unintentionally discharge and possibly kill children. For example, more than 600 people, including children, have been killed or injured by unintentional discharges from Sturm, Ruger's Old Model Single Action Revolver, manufactured from 1953 until 1972. The gun had no positive safety device and was extremely likely to fire when dropped or bumped until it was modified in 1973. By that time, however, consumers had purchased more than 1.5 million of the original revolvers. Sturm, Ruger did not take any action to remedy the hazard posed by the Old Models for another ten years, when the company offered to retrofit Old Models with a transfer bar safety. Unfortunately, only a fraction of the guns have been modified. Despite Sturm, Ruger's knowledge of the defect in the design of the Old Model, the company has not issued a recall of the guns. Even though the guns are old, they still cause death and serious injury. For example, in 1990, Andrew Baxter, a minor, was shot in the abdomen when his father's Old Model unintentionally discharged.

The Remington Model 700

Several other guns have acquired a reputation for being defective, but the most famous example is probably the Remington Model 700 rifle. The Remington Model 700 is one of the best-selling bolt-action rifles in America, with more than 3 million sold since it went on the market in 1962. In the 1990s, it was revealed that this popular rifle could fire without the trigger being pulled. Sometimes it would discharge merely when the safety was unlocked or the gun was bumped. Remington apparently knew about the problem as early as 1979, yet more than 1,000 cases of premature firing and at least 100 death and injury claims were reported to the company without a recall. In a 1994 lawsuit, Remington paid $17 million ($15 million in punitive damages) to a Texas man whose Model 700 rifle accidentally discharged and shot him in the foot.

Remington denies that its Model 700 rifle, which includes nineteen different variations, is defective in its design, but it has admitted similar problems with the Model 600 rifle, which uses the same fire control system. After settling a case in 1978 with a person who became paralyzed when a Model 600 suddenly discharged, Remington recalled that model.

In 1979, Remington's own tests revealed that about 1 percent of the Model 700 guns could be "tricked" into firing accidentally. By that time, the company had sold 2 million Model 700s. According to company documents, Remington decided against a recall because it "would have

> **FAST FACT**
>
> In 1993, eleven-year-old Hank Blacksmith was at the home of his friend, Jesse Coonfare, in Billings, Montana. Coonfare got his father's Remington Model 600 Mohawk rifle, a gun that Remington had recalled in 1978. The gun slipped from Coonfare's hands and accidentally discharged, killing Blacksmith. The ensuing court case was settled out of court in 1996.

to gather 2 million guns just to find 20,000 that are susceptible to this condition." A recall would be extraordinarily costly to the company. No federal agency could require a recall, because guns and tobacco are the only consumer products not subject to federal health and safety regulation.

This Remington 700, known for its "trick" firing, was found among the firearms belonging to a man later convicted in several shooting deaths.

In 1982, faced with increasing numbers of lawsuits, Remington modified the rifle to reduce the likelihood of a malfunction. Nonetheless, suits continued to be filed against the company. In 1988, Brock Aleksich of Butte, Montana, was operating the safety of a Remington Model 700 rifle when the gun discharged and shot his brother Brent in both legs. The teenager suffered severe and permanent physical injuries. The case was settled out of court, and the parties were not allowed to discuss the terms of the settlement.

In October 2000, nine-year-old Gus Barber was shot and killed on a family hunting trip in Montana. The boy's mother was unloading her Remington Model 700, and the gun accidentally discharged, even though her finger was not on the trigger; the bullet went through the wall of a horse trailer and hit her son in the abdomen as he stood on the other side. Her husband bitterly remarked, "My son is a statistic. He was one of 20,000 potential problems Remington knew about."

Not everyone saw the situation like that. One writer for a hunting magazine stated that "the shooting of that boy was not an accident, but a case of severe negligence on the part of the boy's mother.... If handled properly, no firearm really needs a safety—as long as it's never pointed at something that you're not willing to destroy, it will never kill anyone or anything 'accidentally.'"

As a result of Gus Barber's death, Remington admitted in 2002 that it was "aware of reports that rifles...have accidentally discharged while being unloaded, and whenever a gun fires accidentally, there is a risk of property damage, serious injury or death." The "safety modification program" that Remington offered in response, however, was unlike the standard recall practices of federally regulated products. Remington's program did not use the word "recall," was valid for only nine months, and charged consumers twenty dollars. Gus Barber's father, who had been lobbying for a recall, stressed repeatedly that this was not an anti-gun issue. "It's a gun-safety issue," he said. For twelve years, he and his family had been happy with the Remington Model 700: "It would [outshoot] anything that came out of the box. It was a very accurate weapon for my family."

Children and Gun Safety Lawsuits

If a defective product causes an injury, the injured person can sue the manufacturer in a court of law to collect damages. However, American negligence law (known as torts) also holds that the producers of items can be held responsible for products that are defective in design, regardless of whether or not they malfunction. Beginning in the 1990s, some people began to apply this principle to gun manufacturers. They sued firearms companies for damages resulting from defective weapons. They also accused gun manufacturers of failing to include possible safety devices on guns to prevent injuries caused by the foreseeable use or even the foreseeable misuse of guns—for

A member of the Lake Worth, Florida, police department holds up a Raven handgun. The efficacy and safety of the Raven are in question.

example, if a gun was found by a child. These lawsuits against the gun industry were extremely controversial.

Negligence law also recognizes the importance of responsible individual behavior. Guns are a legal product; is the firearms industry really responsible for the misuse of its product by a minority of gun owners? The firearms industry and its supporters argued that gun safety lawsuits use children as propaganda pawns as part of a plot to regulate guns more strictly or ban guns entirely.

One case involved twelve-year-old Ross Mathieu. He was shot and killed by his best friend, who took a Beretta pistol from his father's closet, removed the magazine, aimed the gun at the sixth-grader's head, and pulled the trigger. He was unaware that the gun still had a round in

Former representative Pat Schroeder, a Democrat from Colorado, looking on at a 1996 news conference while a Colt Manufacturing executive explains the company's plans for the smart gun.

its chamber and that the pistol did not have a magazine disconnect safety device, a chamber-loaded indicator, or a locking device. The case was settled one day before the trial was to begin.

In another case, *Halliday v. Sturm, Ruger,* a mother brought a products liability lawsuit against Sturm, Ruger, the manufacturer of a handgun that killed her three-year-old son. On June 6, 1999, Jordan Garris found his father's gun hidden under a mattress and an ammunition magazine on a nearby shelf. Jordan apparently knew how to load the magazine from watching television. He loaded the gun and fatally shot himself. The gun did not have any of the safety features that would have prevented Jordan from being able to fire the gun. The case was never seriously considered by any Maryland courts and was dismissed without coming to trial. The Maryland Court of Appeals declared:

> There was no malfunction of the gun; regrettably, it worked exactly as it was designed and intended to work and as any ordinary consumer would have expected it to work. The gun is a lawful weapon and was lawfully sold. What caused this tragedy was the carelessness of Jordan's father in leaving the weapon and the magazine in places where the child was able to find them, in contravention not only of common sense but of multiple warnings given to him at the time of purchase.

The case of *Smith v. Bryco Arms* took a somewhat different turn. In 1993, fourteen-year-old Sean Smith was with a group of friends when one of the boys removed the ammunition magazine from a semiautomatic handgun. Another boy, believing the gun to be unloaded, fired it toward Sean, unintentionally shooting him in the face. In 2001, two different New Mexico courts allowed the case to go to trial. They ruled that gun makers could be held liable for failing to include feasible safety devices and endangering children by then selling these handguns to

FAST FACT

One critic of the New Mexico Supreme Court's decision in *Smith v. Bryco Arms* wrote, "When will people realize education and training would prevent the majority of these accidents? I say place the responsibility where it belongs and hold owners [responsible]. Teach your kids not to touch guns without adult supervision and don't hand a gun to someone that doesn't know how to use it."

the general public. The New Mexico Court of Appeals stated that Smith's legal team had presented

> straightforward assertions that the handgun could have—and therefore should have—incorporated long-known design features which would have prevented this shooting and others like it.... [the] fact that handguns are meant to fire projectiles which can cause great harm is to our view all the more reason to allow the tort system to assess whether the product is reasonably designed to prevent or help avoid unintended—albeit careless— firings such as occurred here.... We do not perceive anything so unique about handguns that they cannot or should not be subject to normal tort law concepts, norms, and methods of analysis.

Smart Guns

Gun makers are currently developing "smart guns," also known as personalized guns, firearms that can be fired only by a weapon's authorized user. If these designs are successful, they would probably reduce the possibility of accidental firearms injuries to young children and adolescent suicides. In addition, teenagers and others who stole guns would no longer be able to use them. (An estimated 500,000 guns are stolen from homes each year.)

Smart guns attempt to personalize guns in a number of different ways, including the use of magnetic devices, radio frequency transponders, fingerprint identification, and technologies that rely on the authorized user's unique physical characteristics. Taurus International, a leading gun maker, began working with the New Jersey Institute of Technology to develop a smart gun that would use sensors in a gun's grip wired to a microchip inside the gun. The owner would have to have his or her grip programmed at a gun shop or police range by practice-firing the gun. The chip would then "remember" an individual owner's handgrip and prevent the gun from firing if a child or

anyone else attempted to use it. Effective smart guns would be safer than trigger locks and other removable devices because they would provide automatic protection; the gun would normally be in a locked position.

Some states have passed laws imposing smart gun safety standards on gun manufacturers. New York, for example, approved legislation in 2000 directing the state police and other agencies to conduct a study of the availability and effectiveness of existing personalized gun technology. Maryland adopted a similar law in the same year, requiring the Handgun Roster Board to review the status of such technology annually and report its findings to the governor and general assembly.

Douglas Weiss, a technician on the smart gun project at Sandia National Laboratories, holds up a prototype of a smart gun and the computer chip that will be embedded in the gun. The chip corresponds to a pea-size transmitter the owner/operator wears on the wrist. Without the transmitter, the gun cannot be fired.

New Jersey governor James McGreevey (right) points to the handle of a smart gun with grip recognition technology. Democratic officials gathered in early 2004 at the New Jersey Institute of Technology to announce a $1.1 million federal grant to improve and speed up advances in smart gun technology.

In December 2002, New Jersey became the first state to pass smart gun legislation that would eventually require all new handguns to have some mechanism that would allow only their owners to fire them. The law states that all handguns sold in New Jersey must have smart gun technology three years after the state's attorney general declares that a smart gun prototype is safe and commercially available. Personalized handguns will be deemed available for retail sales purposes if at least one manufacturer has delivered at least one production model (not a prototype) of such a handgun to a licensed wholesale or retail dealer in New Jersey or any other state. Opponents of the New Jersey law argued that it made no sense to pass legislation on technology that doesn't exist yet.

So far, the technology does not exist to make completely foolproof personalized guns commercially available at a reasonable price. If it did, gun manufacturers would undoubtedly attempt to capitalize on the beneficial safety features, especially for households with children. Because the American market for guns is becoming saturated, the best way for manufacturers to get new sales is by producing new things. As one gun owner pointed out,

> I have a Glock 9 millimeter handgun which should last many decades; why would I buy anything new? Well, if the industry offers a gun that's much safer, and that would let both me and my wife (who's less comfortable with guns than I am) be less worried about our child accidentally misusing the gun, then I'll definitely buy one.

In 2000, Smith & Wesson was the largest handgun manufacturer in the United States, producing more than 20 percent of the nation's handguns. In March, the company made a voluntary deal with the U.S. government, agreeing to a series of safety and business practice reforms. Among other things, Smith & Wesson agreed that within two years it would include in every firearm it manufactures "a built-in, on-board locking system, by which the firearm can only be operated with a key or combination or other mechanism unique to the gun." Smith & Wesson further stated that within three years it would incorporate in all new firearms designs a form of technology "that recognizes only authorized persons." Although Smith & Wesson's deal with the government quickly fell apart (for other reasons), the agreement seemed to imply that gun manufacturers were at least close to having the ability to design guns that could not be fired by children or other unauthorized users.

FAST FACT

Commenting on smart gun technology, the general manager of the gun company Sturm, Ruger noted, "There is zero room for error here. If you swipe your ATM card and it doesn't read it, do it again. But if you reach for your gun to defend yourself and it doesn't recognize your identification, you don't get a second chance."

Keeping Your Family Safe?

In an educational brochure for parents, *Keep Your Family Safe from Firearm Injury,* the AAP recommends that "[because] even the most well-behaved children are curious by nature and will eagerly explore their environment, the safest thing is to not keep a gun at home." While this doctors' advice might make sense in a perfect world, it ignores the desire of gun owners to have their firearms readily available for self-defense. The approximately 1,500 American children under age eighteen who have been annually killed by firearms in recent years are real enough, but the way to "protect children" to avoid these tragedies in the future remains disputed.

GUN SAFETY

Below is the actual wording pertaining to smart guns in the agreement between Smith & Wesson and the government in 2000.

All handguns must meet the following safety and design standards:

- Second "hidden" serial number, to prevent criminals from obliterating serial numbers.
- External locking device sold with all guns within 60 days.
- Internal locking device on all guns within 24 months.
- Smart Guns—Authorized User Technology.
- Manufacturers commit 2 percent of annual firearms revenues to the development of authorized user technology.
- Within 36 months, authorized user technology will be included in all *new* firearm models, with the exception of curios and collectors' firearms.
- If the top eight manufacturers agree, authorized user technology will be included in *all* new firearms.
- Child Safety. Within 12 months, handguns will be designed so they cannot be readily operated by a child under 6.
- Performance test. All firearms will be subject to a performance test to ensure safety and quality.
- Drop test. All firearms will be subject to a test to ensure they do not fire when dropped.

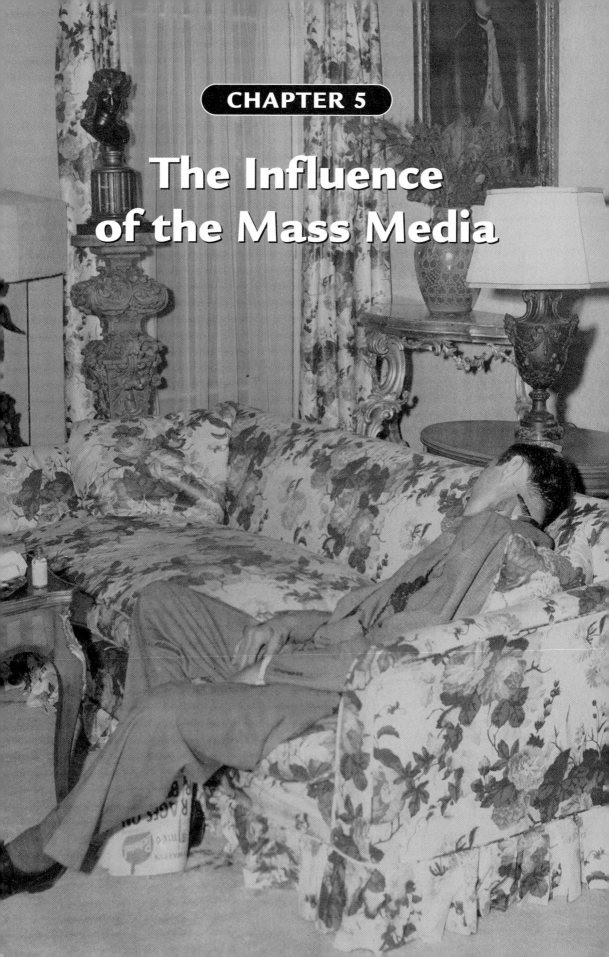

CHAPTER 5

The Influence of the Mass Media

I n 1993, the National Research Council released a report titled *Understanding and Preventing Violence*. In it, the council concluded that "biological, individual, family, peer, school, and community factors may influence the development of an individual potential for violence.... [No] one influence in isolation is likely to account for the development of a potential for violence." Nonetheless, when the United States crime rate goes up or when some horrible multiple-victim school shooting occurs, Americans search for either a reason or a scapegoat. The easy availability of guns has frequently been used to explain the nation's high homicide rate. Recently, this explanation has been replaced by a condemnation of the high level of violence, especially with guns, depicted in American movies, television, music, and video games.

Two seemingly self-evident concepts frame the debate over violence in the American media. Almost no one disputes the power of television and movies to influence Americans' choices. Advertisers (and politicians) would not pay millions of dollars to gain access to people's living rooms if they didn't feel that they could sway people's opinions and change their judgments. On the other hand, very few of the millions of teenagers or adults exposed to violent movies and video games go out and shoot people.

American Mass Media and Violence

Violent behavior has historically appealed to humans—at least while it's being viewed rather than experienced. The Roman Empire sponsored violent duels between people and wild animals in front of roaring crowds. The Aztecs performed human sacrifices as part of their religion and held up the victims' still-beating hearts to the crowds. Punch and Judy, traditional puppet show characters that entranced Europeans for centuries, presented an incredibly violent plot that included the murder of wives and children. Public executions were common throughout the world well into the nineteenth century and remain so in many places.

A group portrait of the real Butch Cassidy (center) and his gang, taken in 1900 shortly after they robbed the bank in Elnnemucca, Nevada. Hollywood portrayed this violent, gunslinging gang with humor and compassion.

In the twenty-first century, the United States lacks official public spectacles of violence, unless one counts professional wrestling or sports such as football and hockey. It is, however, filled with extremely high levels of fictional violence in television, music, video games, comic books, radio broadcasts, magazines, and movies. The problem of violence in the media arises primarily because children spend more time each week consuming American entertainment—especially television—than any other activity except sleeping. The typical child in the United States watches twenty-eight hours of television a week. Ninety-nine percent of American households have at least one television, and more than half of children under age eighteen have televisions in their bedrooms that permit them to watch unsupervised.

At any given moment, television may or may not be depicting violence, but over time, the sheer quantity of television viewing among American children is bound to

FAST FACT

Music videos average more than one violent scene per minute—more than twice the level of either movies or television.

include some violence. By the sixth grade, the average American child has witnessed more than 8,000 television murders and 100,000 other acts of television violence. These numbers don't include violent acts in video games, movies, and other media. By age sixteen, a youngster will have seen 16,000 simulated murders and 200,000 acts of violence. A study in the *Journal of the American Medical Association* claimed that American children see 40,000 murders on a television or movie screen by the time they graduate from high school.

An Old Complaint

Guns and violence have been a staple of American movies and television almost from the invention of the technology. Western cowboys, urban gangsters, and courageous soldiers are among the most traditional characters in American movies and television shows, and they have been popular for more than a century. For

The motion picture industry has also glorified bank robbers Bonnie Parker (left) and Clyde Barrow, who were finally ambushed by police in 1934 after a long career of robbery and murder.

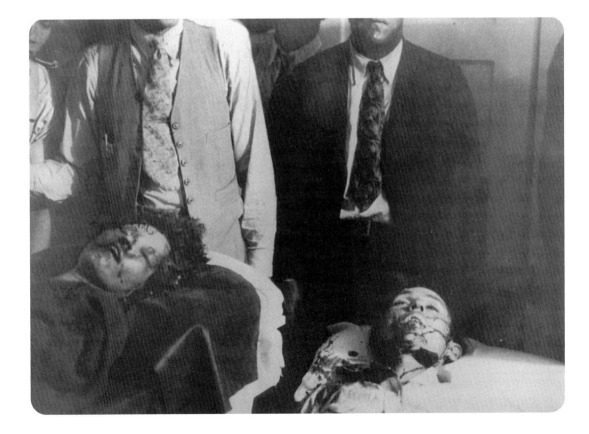

almost the same length of time, some Americans have been outraged over what they considered overly high levels of gratuitous violence and lawlessness in the movies. As early as the 1910s, the government, private organizations, and public boards tried to control movies, condemning the glorification of on-screen criminals and claiming that their illegal actions might inspire similar actions off the screen, especially among young people.

As a result, Hollywood studios established the Production Code Administration (PCA) in 1934 to make rules for all films. The code stated that because movies "are the most popular of modern arts for the masses, [they] have their moral quality from the intention of the minds which produce them and from their effects on the moral lives and reactions of their audiences." Therefore, it was important that in movies, "law, natural or human, shall not be ridiculed," "correct standards of life…shall be presented," and the "sympathy of the audience shall never be thrown to the side of crime, wrong-doing, evil or sin." From 1934 to 1968, the production code was strictly enforced; the American movie industry bent over backward to glorify the Federal Bureau of Investigation (FBI), lawmen, and cowboys. Guns and violence were acceptable to censors, as long as the good guys won.

Bonnie and Clyde, released in 1967, probably represents a watershed in the depiction of guns, violence, and criminals in American films. The Depression-era gangsters were portrayed in the film as lighthearted and funny victims of cold-blooded law enforcers; violence in the film was graphic, sometimes shown in slow motion. The production code was abolished the next year when the popularity of television and foreign films forced Hollywood to become more daring to attract viewers. It was replaced in the late 1960s by a voluntary rating system that has always seemed far more concerned with sexual content than levels of violence on-screen. This ratings system has been adjusted several times into its current form.

> **FAST FACT**
>
> Americans have been concerned with violence in the media long before television. In the 1800s, many social reformers complained that children were imitating the violence that they read about in newspapers.

However, parental warnings and violence advisories for movies often seem to attract more adolescent viewers than they discourage. Studies have shown that "PG" (parental guidance advised), "PG-13" (parental guidance for those under age thirteen), and "R" (restricted to those under seventeen) ratings significantly increased boys' interest in such shows, although they did tend to make girls less interested in watching.

Guns in the Movies and Television

Gun violence ebbs and flows from year to year in movies and television and is extraordinarily hard to measure objectively. Obvious questions arise about the context of violence: What if the "good guy" does it? What if there are negative consequences? What if the violence is historical, as in a depiction of a Civil War battle or of Roman gladiators? Nonetheless, several groups attempt to measure the levels of violence in popular entertainment, albeit imperfectly.

According to a study on television violence administered by the University of California, Santa Barbara, the context in which violence is portrayed is as important to its impact as the amount of violence. The study concluded that almost half of all television violence took place in children's cartoons, and about two-thirds of children's programming had at least some violent content. More troubling was the fact that three-quarters of the shows with violent content involved no punishment for the violence, and in more than half the violent scenes, the victims were not shown to be experiencing pain. Children's programs were the least likely to show any long-term consequences of violence, and in two-thirds of cases, they portrayed violence in a humorous fashion.

Although gun violence on television and in movies takes place at a rate that far exceeds what most people experience in daily life, it did seem to have decreased in the late 1990s. The Centers for Disease Control (CDC) analyzed twenty-five top-grossing G- or PG-rated films from 1995 through 1997 and found an average of 6.4 people per picture with both a gun and a speaking part. The top twenty-five such films in 2000 contained only 3.4 gun-wielders with speaking parts per film. Of the twenty top-grossing films of 2000, only three (*Mission: Impossible 2, Traffic,* and *The Patriot*) featured a great deal of gun violence. (Of course, that doesn't count the very bloody and very successful *Gladiator,* which depicted Roman-era combat but had no guns.) The top-grossing film of 2000 was Dr. Seuss's nonviolent *How the Grinch Stole Christmas.*

On television, there's probably less violence in the early 2000s than there was in the gun-heavy westerns and cop shows of the 1960s, 1970s, and 1980s, such as *Starsky and Hutch* or *Miami Vice.* Police shows such as *Law & Order, CSI: Crime Scene Investigation,* and *NYPD Blue,* with their constant emphasis on crime, gun play, and dead bodies, remain popular, however. On the other hand, some of the most popular programs of recent years, such as *Seinfeld, Friends, The West Wing,* and *Ally McBeal,* or reality shows

More than 10,000 people lined up in New York City in 2003 to audition for the reality television show, American Idol. Gun safety advocates applaud the downward trend in violence on television and hope it continues to have a positive effect on curtailing the use of firearms among children and young adults.

FAST FACT

Some television shows have focused on the dangers of guns. One episode of *Judging Amy* addressed a father losing custody of his kids because of his careless gun-storage practices. *Family Law* and *7th Heaven* both devoted episodes to the dangerous combination of kids and guns in the home. *Law & Order* criticized the unsafe practices of a gun manufacturer in an episode praised for its quality at the 2000 Emmy Awards.

such as *Survivor* and *Who Wants to Be a Millionaire?* rarely involve violence.

However, violence is often used in promos (advertisements to promote programs or movies) as a hook to entice viewers to watch both the entire announcement and the program that it advertises. Promos have only a very short time to show something interesting enough to attract viewers. With so little time, the easiest things to feature are those that require little explanation: violence and sex. Viewers do not need any context to see that a show will contain action, guns, or fistfights. During the show itself, commercials often interrupt violent scenes or occur just as violence is about to occur, ensuring that viewers will continue watching. These promotional efforts imply that networks believe that violence attracts, not repels, viewers to programs.

Video Games

To a large degree, outright gun violence has migrated to video games, especially those marketed to adolescent males. These extremely violent, bloody games are often among the industry's top sellers. A report in 2001 singled out ten popular video games for criticism because they involved realistic guns and the shooting, killing, and maiming of people. Some of the violent games featuring guns and human victims were *Redneck Rampage, Hitman, Max Payne, Soldier of Fortune, Gangsters 2, Doom 2,* and *Delta Force: Land Warrior.* One analyst complained, "For parents who own guns, these games take all of the lessons that they teach their children about gun safety and throw them out the window." While many of the games carry a box label indicating that they are violent, the labels are merely advisory; unlike movie ratings, they do not even pretend to prevent young children from buying or otherwise gaining access to the games.

Several cities and states have attempted to censor video games, but the courts have not permitted most bans to stand. In 2001, St. Louis, Missouri, banned the sale of

violent video games to minors, but the law was declared unconstitutional by a U.S. appeals court. In 2003, the state of Washington passed a law aimed at keeping children from buying games that depict violence against police. A less controversial (and less effective) solution is a rating system; the Entertainment Software Rating Boards, a U.S. industry group, has been assigning ratings to video games since 1994. Unfortunately, video games have proven no easier to rate than television shows or movies. In 2003, the rating board was forced to add new categories to distinguish between the graphic depictions of blood and gore in games like *Doom* and *Grand Theft Auto: Vice City,* and violence in cartoon-style games (presumably less serious).

Major gun manufacturers, such as Colt, Browning, and Remington, have recognized the popularity of video games among boys and have begun to use video games as marketing tools. The editor of *Guns Magazine* stated, "What we need is a computer game which combines the

Laura Smit, a mother and gun control activist, holds up a realistic-looking gun used for a video game. The Senate Governmental Affairs Committee held hearings in 2001 to determine the effectiveness of the different ratings systems used to indicate levels of sex and violence in movies, music, video games, and television.

use of the real handgun...with state-of-the-art graphics and an exciting story...a game like that would be an extremely effective vehicle to introduce safe recreational shooting to the video games generation." Two hunting games by gun manufacturers, *Remington Upland Game Hunter* and *Browning Duck Hunter,* have been praised for their responsible approach to gun use and gun safety. As of 2002, however, the games were selling poorly—ironically, because they were not violent enough—and some had been taken off the market. Criticism by gun control advocacy groups has caused at least two gun manufacturers to request that their guns not be used in violent games produced by other companies.

After the school massacres of the late 1990s, several analysts noted that many of the school shooters enjoyed playing violent, "first-person shooter" video games, in which the player gets points for shooting almost anything that moves. Both murderers in the Columbine High School massacre in 1999 enjoyed playing *Doom*, a bloody

Jeff Cole, director of the UCLA Center for Communication Policy, shows one of several violent clips used in a study of violence in the media that was funded by the networks.

shooting video game licensed by the U.S. military to train soldiers to kill effectively. One of the killers' personal web sites had a customized version of *Doom* with two shooters who had extra weapons and unlimited ammunition, while the other people in the game couldn't fight back. For a class project, they made a videotape that was similar to their customized version of *Doom*; in the video, they dressed in trench coats, carried guns, and killed school athletes. The pair acted out their videotaped performance in real life less than a year later.

Violent Media Leads to Real-Life Violence

There's not much dispute anymore about the dangers of excessive violence in American mass media. More than 1,000 studies have been done on the influence of media violence on viewers and listeners. The vast majority have concluded that there is a clear link between media violence and aggressive behavior that goes beyond the idea that violent people like to watch violent entertainment. The first major study after the invention of television developed out of the extensive rioting in the 1960s. As a result, President Lyndon Johnson created a National Commission on the Causes and Prevention of Violence and commissioned Gerbner's Cultural Indicators to analyze the content of television shows. This research led to the 1972 U.S. Surgeon General's report that found evidence of "a causal relation between viewing violence on television and aggressive behavior."

In 1982, the U.S. Surgeon General's office again examined the existing research and once again found that televised violence contributed to antisocial behavior. Since then, the American Medical Association (AMA), the American Psychological Association (APA), the National Institute of Mental Health (NIMH), the American Academy of Pediatrics (AAP), and the American Academy of Child and Adolescent Psychiatry unanimously concluded that television violence was a major factor in "real-world" violence. In 1993, the APA claimed that television was responsible for more than 15 percent of the violent behavior in kids.

This position was argued in court when the families of three of the victims in the school shooting in West Paducah, Kentucky, claimed in 1997 that the murderer's actions were inspired by *The Basketball Diaries,* a movie released in 1995. In this film, actor Leonardo DiCaprio's character has a detailed and bloody fantasy vision of going on a shooting spree in his high school. The families sued the makers of the film and its distributors, including Time Warner and Polygram Film Entertainment Distribution; a federal judge dismissed the lawsuit in 2000.

The Problem with Violence in the Media

Obviously, the presence of gun violence in video games, television, and movies is not the only cause of teenage crime and homicide. Defenders of the entertainment industry properly point out that their product is not "real," and viewers know it.

However, supporters of limits to media violence argue that the entertainment industry's glorification of guns and violence affects everyone in several negative ways, especially teenagers who are prone to violent behavior. Watching several gun murders a day on television or shooting a few hundred people in a video game desensitizes the viewer or player to violence. This makes people care less about violence directed at others and makes it less likely that a person would take action to help a victim of violence. Audiences gradually accept increasing levels of on-screen brutality, and ever more graphic depictions are necessary to shock them. In some cases, media violence seems to increase the viewer's appetite for becoming involved with violence. Many people come to believe that shooting someone or something is an ordinary, acceptable way to be entertained, settle arguments, and blow off steam.

Violent behavior is often glorified in American mass media. Kids learn that desirable commodities and personal power can be obtained through the use of aggression. Excessive television viewing and video games have also replaced activities that once might have been shared with family and friends. Viewers of high levels of violence assume that the world is a brutal, scary place and have increased fears of becoming victims of violence. This feeling increases self-protective behaviors and mistrust of others. These viewers tend to own more guns, and their kids feel less safe. Sexual violence in X- and R-rated videotapes, which are widely available to teenagers, has also been linked to an increase in male aggression against females. Some teenagers have been known to mimic the violence that they see on-screen. Two surveys of young American male violent felons found that about a quarter

Violence has become part of the initiation rite that kids must undergo when they seek to become gang members.

had imitated crime techniques that they had watched on television.

The effects of watching violent entertainment are both short-term and long-lasting. A study of boys found a significant relation between exposure to television violence at eight years of age and antisocial acts—including serious, violent criminal offenses and spousal abuse—twenty-two years later. A similar study in 2003 reexamined the lives of several hundred people in the Chicago area who, as children aged six to ten, had taken part in a 1977 study. The result showed that men who were high television-violence viewers as children were much more likely than others to have abused their wives, to have responded to insults by shoving a person, and to have been convicted of a crime. The researchers concluded that childhood exposure to media violence could actually predict adult aggressive behavior.

Possible Solutions

A solution implies a problem, and for First Amendment purists, there's no problem at all with violence in the media, even when it comes to "protecting children." These people believe that, except in rare cases, free speech should not be infringed and that the answer to violent speech is more speech. They concede that there may be some link between media violence and actual violence, but insist that only an extremely small minority of the audience for television, music, movies, and video games ever commits a crime. The vast majority simply prefers violent entertainment because it is exciting.

Some of those in favor of the opposite position support some sort of government or industry organization censoring the entertainment industry based on the content of each production. Some groups have supported a boycott against studios or advertisers associated with extremely violent programming. This strategy seems unlikely to be effective, given the

acceptance of many forms of violent entertainment in the United States.

Many people believe that the vast popularity of violence in American movies, music, video games, and television is simply a reflection of American society; in this view, Americans hypocritically condemn violent programming while continuing to purchase the product. One cynical commentator remarked,

> Violent and stupid entertainment is popular because it corresponds to reality which is often violent and stupid.... Take a society in which half the population is armed; with astronomical rates of rape, domestic violence, child abuse and

The struggle for a thorough ratings system for different media has been lengthy. In this 1999 photograph, Senator Orrin Hatch, a Republican from Utah, holds up a compact disc recorded by Marilyn Manson, a popular musician who many adults believe inspires violence in children who listen to the music.

FAST FACT

As far back as 2,500 years ago, the Greek philosopher Plato, in his book *The Republic,* supported censoring artists in order to protect the morals of children:

We must...forbid [craftsmen] to represent the evil disposition, the licentious, the illiberal, the graceless, either in the likeness of living creatures or in any other product of their art among us, that our guardians may not be bred among symbols of evil, as it were, in a pasturage of poisonous herbs, lest grazing freely and cropping from many such day by day they little by little and all unawares accumulate and build up a huge mass of evil in their own souls.

murder...in which people are told they should be able to have whatever they want, but only if they can pay for it and if they can't they're losers. Why wouldn't the inhabitants of such a society thrill to watch their psychosocial dramas enacted on screen?

Some organizations attempt to chart a middle course between the First Amendment and censorship by lobbying entertainment producers, publicizing (and shaming) inappropriate cultural products, and attempting to educate the public about the importance of supervising content in the programs that children watch. The Parents Television Council (PTC), Preview Family Movie and TV Review Online, and the National Institute on Media and the Family represent some of the organizations that judge the violence quotient of the entertainment industries. The PTC has more than half a million members, strong grassroots chapters, and an advisory board filled with well-known celebrities.

The so-called V-chip is yet another way of preventing children from viewing violence, at least on television. The V-chip, a device that can block the display of violent programs, allows parents a way to control what television programs can be seen in their homes without the need to constantly supervise the viewing habits of their children. Since January 2000, all new television sets with screens 13 inches (33 centimeters) or larger have included V-chip technology. The V-chip can also be purchased as an add-on device. In the beginning years of the twenty-first century, however, use of the V-chip has not been widespread, partly because of the novelty of the technology and partly because many parents apparently don't care as much as some people think they should about what their children watch.

Another difficulty for television has been the constructing of a workable ratings system for an estimated 600,000 hours of programming broadcast per year (based on a seventy-channel cable system). Hollywood, in contrast, has to rate roughly 550 movies (1,000 hours) per year. The problem of applying meaningful violence ratings and/or blocking certain television programming was immense, given the range of television shows as varied as crime-filled local news, professional wrestling, *ER,* Three Stooges reruns, and Power Rangers cartoons. At present, most ratings guidelines are based on age instead of content. This can make it difficult for parents to decide what content is appropriate for their children to view, since children vary widely in their intelligence and maturity at any age.

Lawrence Lien, head of Parental Guide Inc., explains how the V-chip can block viewers from watching television programs containing violence and other inappropriate material.

The Telecommunications Act of 1996

Complaints about the media glorification of guns and violence are often their loudest during periods when the crime rate is high or after dramatic school shootings. When levels of violent youth crime peaked in the early 1990s, Congress felt obligated to act because, as it reported,

President Bill Clinton signs the Telecommunications Act in 1996. Despite good intentions, domestic policy has not focused on the development or enforcement of many of the bill's directives.

television influences children's perception of the values and behavior that are common and acceptable in society.... There is a compelling governmental interest in empowering parents to limit the negative influences of video programming that is harmful to children. Providing parents with timely information about the nature of upcoming

video programming and with the technological tools that allow them easily to block violent, sexual, or other programming that they believe harmful to their children is a nonintrusive and narrowly tailored means of achieving that compelling governmental interest.

In 1996, Congress passed the Telecommunications Act. Title V of this act is titled "Obscenity and Violence" and is also referred to as the Communications Decency Act (CDA). This legislation required the television industry to develop a voluntary ratings system. In addition, the act required that by the year 2000, all televisions manufactured in the United States would contain the V-chip.

In June 1997, the U.S. Supreme Court ruled unanimously that parts of the CDA were an unconstitutional violation of the First Amendment. Writing for the Court, Justice John Paul Stevens held that

> in the absence of evidence to the contrary, we presume that governmental regulation of the content of speech is more likely to interfere with the free exchange of ideas than to encourage it. The interest in encouraging freedom of expression in a democratic society outweighs any theoretical but unproven benefit of censorship.

A Temporary Lull?

Shortly after the Telecommunications Act was passed, the wave of highly publicized school shootings began in Pearl, Mississippi; West Paducah, Kentucky; Jonesboro, Arkansas; Springfield, Oregon; and Littleton, Colorado. As usual, many analysts found fault with the products of the American entertainment industry and blamed movies, television, and video games for American violence.

In the absence of any major multiple-victim school shootings in the early twenty-first century, however, other issues took precedence: the election of 2000, the recession, the terrorist attack on the United States in 2001, and the 2003 war in Iraq. Nonetheless, the issue of gun violence in the media is unlikely to go away, and it will assuredly rise again when the next disaster like the Columbine massacre occurs.

Glossary

advocacy group—an organization that seeks to persuade people to support a particular viewpoint on a public issue, such as for or against increased restrictions on gun use

amendment—a change or addition to a legal document, such as an amendment to the U.S. Constitution

assault weapons—antipersonnel rifles, shotguns, and handguns designed mainly for military and law enforcement purposes

caliber—a measurement of the inside of a gun barrel

cartridge—a case that holds the primer and bullet; also, the case, primer, and bullet all together

commerce clause—a clause in the U.S. Constitution that empowers Congress to act in matters involving trade between the states

crime rate—the amount of crime, presented in statistical terms

firearm—a weapon that uses a powder charge to shoot something, usually a bullet or shell, from a straight tube

gun control—restrictions on the use and ownership of guns

homicide—murder

liability—legal obligation or responsibility

magazine—the container in a firearm that stores the cartridges before they pass into the chamber for firing; also a storehouse for gunpowder and ammunition

police power—the power of a government to preserve public order and maintain minimum standards of health, safety, and welfare for its citizens

poll—a sampling of public opinion

round—a single shot from a firearm; a cartridge

school zone—as designated by law, a geographic area around a school in which firearms are strictly regulated

self-defense—an action by an individual to protect himself or herself

semiautomatic weapon—a weapon that reloads automatically after firing, although the trigger must be pulled to fire each round; different from an automatic weapon, which fires more than one round with a single pull of the trigger

smart gun—a firearm equipped with technology that allows it to be used only by a specific individual

suicide—the taking of one's own life

trigger lock—a device incorporated into a firearm to prevent its accidental firing

Bibliography

Books

Capozzoli, Thomas, and R. Steve McVey. *Kids Killing Kids: Managing Violence and Gangs in Schools.* Boca Raton, FL: St. Lucie Press, 2000.

Dizard, Jan, et al. *Guns in America: A Reader.* New York: New York University Press, 1999.

Grapes, Bryan, ed. *School Violence.* San Diego: Greenhaven Press, 2000.

National Research Council Institute of Medicine. *Deadly Lessons: Understanding Lethal School Violence.* Washington, DC: National Academies Press, 2003.

Shafii, Mohammed, and Sharon Shafii, eds. *School Violence: Assessment, Management, Prevention.* Washington, DC: American Psychiatric Publishing, 2001.

Spitzer, Robert. *The Politics of Gun Control.* 2nd ed. New York: Chatham House, 1998.

U.S. Congress. House Committee on the Judiciary, Subcommittee on Crime and Criminal Justice. *Caught in the Crossfire: Kids Talk about Guns.* Washington, DC: United States Government Printing Office, 1995.

Utter, Glenn. *Encyclopedia of Gun Control and Gun Rights.* Phoenix: Oryx Press, 2000.

Watson, Rollin, and Robert Watson. *The School as Safe Haven.* Westport, CT: Bergin and Garvey, 2002.

Web Sites

The Brady Campaign to Prevent Gun Violence
United with the Million Mom March
www.handguncontrol.org

Common Sense about Kids and Guns
www.kidsandguns.org/study/web_resources.asp?topic=Schools

Entertainment Industries Council (EIC) Online—Gun Violence, Safety & Injury Prevention Resource Center *eiconline.org/violence/*

Firearms Law Center *www.firearmslawcenter.org/content/home.asp*

The Future of Children—Protecting Children from the Harmful Effects of Gun Violence *www.futureofchildren.org/information2827/ information_show.htm?doc_id=154462*

National Rifle Association (NRA) *www.nra.org*

Office of Juvenile Justice and Delinquency Prevention (OJJDP)—School Violence Resources *ojjdp.ncjrs.org/resources/school.html*

U.S. Department of Justice—Bureau of Justice Statistics (BJS) *www.ojp.usdoj.gov/bjs/welcome.html*

Index

Note: Page numbers in *italics* indicate illustrations and captions.